Complete Bicycle
Time Trialing Book

Complete Bicycle Time Trialing Book

from the editors of Bike World Magazine

World Publications

Box 366, Mountain View, CA 94042

© 1977 by
World Publications
Box 366, Mountain View, CA 94042

*No information in this book may be reprinted in
any form without permission from the publisher.*

Library of Congress 77-85324
ISBN 0-89037-123-7

Foreword

The urge for competition might be there, but the opportunity could be missing. Many cyclists in this nation have experienced this phenomenon, especially if they are riding out of love for cycling and not to make a living.

Time trial riding provides the missing opportunity, not only for the casual cyclist but also for the avid racer. Time trialing is for everyone, and can be used in a variety of ways from filling a Sunday afternoon to training for a national championship.

What has tied the racer and the casual cyclist together all these years is a common love for cycling. Time trials in the past have been viewed only as an event for an avid racer who has the time for training and the equipment for winning. Even though the two groups of cyclists have been separated by this elusive opportunity to participate in the same events (but on differing levels), the separation today seems minimal.

In time trialing, the competition is not directly against fellow cyclists, even though results from the actual running of the time trial could be considered competition among cyclists. During the actual running of the time trial, however, the only adversary is the clock. Racers, casual cyclists, tourists, commuters and even the kid on the "banana seat special" all can participate in time trialing. Each is racing to beat the clock.

The results of the time trials offer further possibilities to riders. As times are compared for common distances (one of the most appealing of which is 25 miles) and are compiled, a commuter from New Jersey can see how he fared against a commuter in London merely by comparing times.

Through time trialing, all cyclists can now satisfy that recurring urge for competition. Through time trialing, all cyclists are able to improve their cycling abilities while satisfying that urge. Through time trialing, all cyclists are able to care for their obvious first loves, cycling.

Through the efforts of such publications as this booklet and *Bike World* magazine, time trialing is gaining the popularity in this country that it has enjoyed in European countries for years. Each of the contributors to this book should be given a note of thanks.

William Sanders, contributing editor for *Bike World* (in which his column "At the Starting Line" is a regular feature), offers some excellent opening remarks about the sport of time trialing and some good advice about equipment.

John Wilcockson, international editor for *Bike World* (and author of the column "News from Europe"), shows how the look of time trials has changed and improved through the years.

Martyn Roach is a familiar name to those who have followed the European racing scene. An internationally-known time trialist and someone familiar with the taste of victory, Roach has some interesting advice.

Jim Harper is the chairman of the US Cycling Federation's national championship committee and explains how to measure accurately a course for your club's time trials. Other contacts for information about the USCF and a list of official rules (in laymen's terms) are included.

Lyn Lemaire is most recently acclaimed for her first place finish among the senior women in the 1976 National Time Trial Championships sponsored by the USCF. Simon Leigh is a regular contributor to *Bike World* and shares some of his tips to better time trialing. Cy and Marge Campbell are contributors to *BW* who share some information about timing and developments in that area of the sport.

And, of course, our thank-you's would not be complete without a nod of approval to all of the photographers who have contributed to this booklet.

Contents

Introduction by William Sanders

Why time trial? Isn't it really pretty much of a dead end and a blind alley for the competitive cyclist? Isn't it far too technical, and too physically demanding for anyone but a handful of superjocks? And isn't it true that all but a few oddballs find they hate it, and that it bores normal people? Who needs it, and why?

FOR THE RACER

A few years ago an American road racer could reasonably say (as many did), "Why should I fool around with time trials? There aren't enough of them to really get into it, you never get any recognition unless you set a record or something and prizes are nonexistent."

Today all this has changed—time trialing has become an accepted branch of cycling. Any club that neglects to promote time trials along with their other events cannot pretend to have a balanced program, and a road racer who can't cope with the time trial has little chance of rising to the top.

In part, the turnabout has been because of the establishment of the National Time Trial Championship, with a status equal to that of any other national championship, including the awarding of the coveted stars-and-stripes jersey. To win this would be, in itself, the realization of most cyclist's dreams. But there is a stronger reason for taking time trials seriously: stage racing.

In the last couple of years stage racing has become *the* status branch of US cycling, attracting the biggest prize lists, the heaviest publicity and the attention of talent-hunting international coaches. And any stage race worthy of the name will include a time trial stage in which one can pick up or drop enough time to affect final, overall placing.

For those who entertain no thought of winning national

titles or competing in stage races, however, there are still plenty of reasons to work on time trialing. For one, time trialing is a splendid form of training. Not only is the aerobic workout beneficial, but the precise time measurement will indicate your progress as well.

Beginning racers will find that time trialing, demanding less tactical expertise and bike handling ability, offers a good chance to measure oneself against higher-ranked riders without the physical hazards involved in racing with a large pack. And finally, time trialing gives the ability to maintain the long, solo breaks that are very useful in road racing.

FOR THE TOURIST

Many casual riders wonder how they would fare in competition, but hesitate to go the full racing route. Time trialing is perfectly suitable to them.

The whole point of a time trial is to ride at your own best speed; there's nobody pulling at your jersey and yelling for you to get out of the way, or making loud cracks about "letting all these turkeys into the race."

There is, in fact, a long-standing tradition that all times and all riders are to be respected. The putdowns encountered in racing are relatively rare among time trialists. Only the cheating rider is looked down upon.

Apart from all these incentives, however, there are more positive reasons for the non-racer to take up time trialing. For physical fitness alone, it would be worth doing. Time trialing involves steady-state, aerobic exertion over a period of an hour or so, without any sudden sprints or jumps that might overload the cardiovascular system. This, of course, is one of the main reasons time trialing is so popular with older riders, but younger riders also should consider this. In addition, leg injuries seem less common in time trialing and time trial training, perhaps because of the smoother, steadier pedaling involved.

The rider with limited time will find time trialing has certain special advantages. Most events are short, usually 25 miles or even 10. Obviously, it takes less time daily to train for a 25-mile event than for long-distance road racing or even long-range touring. This is a real "plus" for those who have to work long hours or attend late classes.

Riders of all ages have participated in time trials. Crippled persons, deaf persons and riders with numerous other handicaps have been able to time trial. There should be no reason why anyone could not take part, assuming basic physical fitness.

Get a physical before taking up time trialing at *any* level. If you cycle at speeds below 15 m.p.h., you might have some problems that still have not surfaced, and a 25-mile fast ride might bring them out in a sudden and dangerous manner.

Time trialing also should be avoided by people who think only easy things are worth doing. It's enjoyable, yes, but not easy. It demands self-discipline and great concentration. There's no one around to talk you into staying with it or make diverting conversation; there is just you, your bike and the road, and somewhere, a watch ticking away the minutes.

THE ESSENTIALS

Bidlake's Brillance:
A Short History
by John Wilcockson

Time trialing started almost by accident. From the time that bicycle racing originated in Europe in 1869, events were held on a massed-start basis—first as short sprints and later over longer distances on the open road.

In the quest for greater speed, racers in England were paced by relays of support riders. But by the late 19th Century, cyclists were beginning to compete for road space with motorized traffic, and this led to congestion. There were public complaints, the police stopped some races and more than one racer was cited.

Cycling's administrators terminated road racing, transferring the events to the many velodromes that England boasted at the time. The only bicycle sport left on British roads was place-to-place and long-distance record riding—strictly controlled, lone record attempts against the clock. These efforts were, in effect, time trials, but included no competitive element—there was only the challenge to beat the time set by another lone rider on a previous day. And riders were still being paced by other cyclists.

Record attempts became popular with racers who had once taken part in massed start events, so in 1888 the Road Records Association was established to keep a proper check on the various attempts. The first records to be recognized were for 50 miles, 100 miles, 24 hours and the 850-mile Land's End to John O'Groats race.

Records were recognized for four separate classes—bicycles, tricycles, tandems and tandem tricycles. One successful rider was F.T. Bidlake of the North Road Cycling Club, who set the tricycle records for 50 miles, 100 miles, 12 hours, 24 hours and London-York in 1895. He wanted to bring back some form of competition to road cycling.

The result was a brilliant idea by Bidlake to eliminate both paced riding and direct racing, but to introduce a competitive element to road sport. A number of racers would be invited to ride, unpaced, over a set course on the same day, with each man starting alone separated by a time interval of at least one minute. Thus, the road time trial was born.

The first recorded time trial was the North Road CC 50-mile event, which took place in October, 1895. It was staged on a course measured out-and-back on the Great North Road, the principal highway running due north out of London. The new form of competition was a success and other open events became established in England—the Anfield BC Invitation 100-mile, the Bath Road "100," the Broad Oak 12-hour and the Catford CC 24-hour, for example.

By this time, racing against the clock had become so popular in England that some form of control was needed to sort out the multitude of events. Organizing clubs met in 1921 to discuss the question, resulting in the formation, in 1922, of the Road Racing Council. It later became the Road Time Trials Council (RTTC) in 1938, when membership became open to every cycling club in England and Wales.

National championships now are held at different locations throughout the racing season—starting with the Men's 25-mile Championship in June ending with the hill climb title race in October.

The most prestigious competition is the British Best All Rounder (BBAR) championship, first organized in 1930 by *Cycling* magazine and run by the RTTC since 1944. The competition is based upon each entrant's fastest performances in any one season at 50 miles, 100 miles and 12 hours. The rider's speed is taken for each of the three events, and the BBAR "speed" is computed as the average of the three.

Throughout the history of time trialing, man has teamed with his bike to realize nature's breathtaking brilliance.

Tim Rivers

The first winner of the BBAR was Frank Southall—the most famous English time trialist of the 1930s. He won the competition four times—a record since equalled by Ken Joy (1949-1952) and Phil Griffiths (1971 and 1974-1976). A three-time winner was Ray Booty, the man who in 1956 became the first time trialist to break through the four-hour barrier at 100 miles. His time was 3:58:28, using a fixed gear of only 84 inches.

It was in 1947 that the 25 m.p.h. standard was first reached at 50 miles (by George Fleming, another famous name in time trialing), while the first sub-hour 25-mile time trial was achieved by Basil Francis in 1940.

At the longer distances, 20 m.p.h. was the important barrier to be beaten. This speed was first achieved at 12 hours in 1928 by Jack Lauterwasser, who rode 75 yards over the 240-mile mark. This was a remarkable performance at a time when road pavements were rudimentary and when racers had to wear (under RTTC non-publicity rules) black tights and button-up jackets. At 24 hours, Denis White was the first to reach the magic 20 m.p.h. mark, when he covered 484.64 miles in a day in 1956.

In the '60s and '70s, smoother pavements, lighter equipment and the use of derailleur gears all were factors that contributed to faster times. It has been said also that another important factor was the growing use of busy divided highways as time trial courses. But this is a controversial subject that is still un-resolved in British time trialing.

The various British men's time trial records, at the beginning of 1977, were as follows:

EVENT	RIDER	RECORD	SPEED
10 miles	Willi Moore	20:36	29.126
25 miles	Alf Engers	51:00	29.431
30 miles	Alf Engers	1:02:27	28.823
50 miles	John Watson	1:43:46	28.911
100 miles	Phil Griffiths	3:46:22	26.505
12 hours	John Watson	281.77 miles	23.481
24 hours	Roy Cromack	507.00 miles	21.150
100k	London West	2:07:52	29.157

These are the principal distances for road time trialing in Britain, as well as in other countries where British cyclists have helped establish time trial traditions, such as countries in the British Commonwealth.

In the US, 10- and 25-mile events are the most popular, while time trials are also staged at 50 miles, 100 miles, 12 hours and 24 hours in certain areas. The United States Cycling Federation (USCF) is the governing body that ratifies all records—verifying times and distances by accurate measurement. In the annual USCF national championships, time trial titles are contested at 25 miles by men, women, Veterans and Juniors. Senior champions in 1976 were John Howard with a time of 55:37 and Lyn Lemaire with 1:00:07.

The rules of the RTTC (like those of the USCF) are strict when it comes to measurement of distances and times. Courses are normally "out-and-back" on the same length of road (with a U-turn) at 10, 25, 30 and 50 miles. At 100 miles, more than one out-and-back section is used (perhaps with the inclusion of a circuit); while 12- and 24-hour courses normally are combinations of circuits and out-and-back legs, with a finishing circuit of 10-15 miles in length.

Time trials at fixed distances are almost unknown outside the English-speaking world. In fact, very few time trials are held in continental Europe. The most common type is a short stage of 4-40 kilometers, part of a multi-day stage race. For instance, five individual time trials were scheduled for the 1977 Tour de France—8, 30, 13, 50 and 6 kilometers, respectively.

The world's most famed time trial is the classic Grand Prix des Nations, first promoted in 1932. For 40 years, the Nations was held on hilly courses in the Paris area before being transferred to the west of France.

Time trials were not introduced as integral parts of major stage races until after WWII. Since then, they have proved a vital ingredient of these events—revealing the true strengths of men such as Jacques Anquetil and Eddy Merckx, both five-time winners of the Tour de France.

Anquetil's greatest virtue was consistency, which made him one of the best time trialists ever. The son of a Normandy farmer, the blond Frenchman astonished Europe in 1953 when, at the age of 19, he won the Nations in his first race as a professional. The race was then at its most difficult—a very hilly 140-k course—with the previous two winners having been Tour de France winners Louison Bobet and Hugo Koblet.

Anquetil was never beaten in the Nations, winning the event nine times between 1953 and 1966. He still holds the record (at 25 m.p.h.) for the 140-k course.

Two other names in the time trialing hall of fame are the Italians Fausto Coppi and Felice Gimondi, both winners of the Tour de France and Giro d'Italia.

Coppi was virtually unknown outside of Italy when he first traveled to Paris to contest the 1946 Grand Prix des Nations. He *had* won the wartime Giro (in 1940) and broken the world unpaced hour record under Mussolini-inspired secrecy. But the rest of the world was awaiting confirmation of this skinny Italian who had ended the war in a North African prisoner-of-war camp.

The world was not disappointed. Coppi won the 1946 Nations in classic style, repeating his victory in 1947. Twenty years later it was Gimondi who won the French time trial classic, and he too performed the "double." His 1968 average of 29.528 m.p.h. for the 73.5-k course still stands as the fastest Nations on record.

Perhaps the most spectacular time trial race of all is Switzerland's Gran Prix de Lugano. This 77.5-k event—five laps of a hilly circuit—is contested by a select group of invited riders and is watched by a fanatical crowd of more than 50,000. All the great time trialists have raced here, with the record being Eddy Merckx' winning ride of 1968, at 26.65 m.p.h.

The only road time trial at the world championships and Olympics is the amateur 100-k team time trial (75-k for juniors).

This is contested by teams of four riders, three of whom must complete the course. First run at the 1960 Olympics, this grueling event follows the strict rules of individual time trials—but there the similarity ends.

In a team time trial (whether with teams of two, three, four or more), each team member makes a short, fast pull at the front before dropping to the back of the line. He then follows the wheels in front before it is again his turn to make the pace-making effort. In effect, the racer is performing 30 m.p.h. intervals, non-stop, for more than two hours. It is an irregular, demanding effort, totally different from the long, steady pull of the individual time trialist.

In a team time trial, a close understanding between the four riders is essential. It is better to discard one man if he is having a bad day because a well-knit team of three riders will go much faster than one worrying about a "lame dog." And four men of moderate ability usually make a better outfit than four individual aces.

An example of an ideal combination was the Swedish team that won the world championship in 1967, 1968 and 1969. The team was composed of four brothers—Gosta, Sture, Tomas and Erik Pettersson—all of whom were more than six feet tall. They were perfectly matched; their powerful pedaling made them faster than any team yet seen. Their speed was as much because of their well-drilled changes as to the use of very high gears. (They set a trend by riding single chainwheels of 55 or 56 teeth in combination with sprockets of 13-17.)

The most famous professional team time trial race is the two-man Baracchi Trophy. This event brings together the big names of world cycling to do battle over a course of 90-110-k across the north Italian plain, east of Milan. Two of the Swedish Pettersson brothers (Gosta and Tomas) teamed together in

1970 (their first season as professionals) and shattered the race record with a speed of 29.49 m.p.h.

Then, on a shorter course in 1971, the combination of Spaniard Luis Ocana (later to win the Tour de France) and Dane Leif Mortensen (1969 amateur world road champion) smashed the 30 m.p.h. barrier for the first time in the Baracchi. Their record still stands, despite other wins by teams such as Eddy Merckx and Ferdinand Bracke (both holders of the world hour record), as well as the team of Anquetil and Gimondi.

Equipment
For Conscientious Riders by William Sanders

Questions of equipment for time trialing have spurned a great deal of study, experimentation and heated debate ever since the sport was invented. Time trialists, in fact, tend to be the most equipment-conscious of bicycle riders.

Given the nature of the sport, it is easy to see why. As a rule, placings are very close these days. Major events, even a national championship, may be won or lost by fractions of a second. It doesn't take much to make that kind of difference over 25 or even 10 miles, so there is reason to be concerned over details that might seem trivial in other areas of competition.

As a result of this and other factors, it is possible to become involved with highly specialized equipment and modifications to the point of owning some very exotic hardware.

There are special time trial bikes that have no other application. They are as specialized and impractical for any other purpose as a Formula I racing car or a fencing foil.

The existence of such special equipment, however, should not be taken by the beginning time trialist as an indication of what is needed. A great deal depends on the individual—what his reasons are for getting into time trialing and what he wants to get out of it.

There are those who like to time trial without really caring particularly about winning or losing. Their interests lie in improving their own best times, or simply riding hard for the fun of it. For these people, there's little point in worrying about equipment.

On the other hand, the active racing cyclist who already has a good, general purpose road racing bike has a good time trial bike—with a pair of light wheels added and perhaps some changes in gearing.

The only people who really need to consider the pure time

trial bike are those whose interests are in time trialing and nothing else, or riders who time trial enthusiastically but don't care about any other branch of competition. A road racer who rides many time trials or races containing time-trial stages may want to acquire a special bike. (But if you're good enough to need that, you'll be able to find a sponsor who'll give it to you.) However, there's no federal law or US Cycling Federation (USCF) rule that says you can't have one just because you want one. As one old-timer once said to me, "It makes me feel faster, and I figure that helps me go faster."

Whether you want to set up a time-trial-only bike or merely make a few temporary modifications to a regular bike, it may be useful to consider some of the requirements.

FRAMES

Frames present a curious situation. In some ways, time trialing puts less demand on the frame than criterium or road racing: there are no extreme cornering forces or sudden sprints. While the frame does need to be reasonably stiff (you don't want it soaking up a lot of power), the problem of whip is considerably less, and frame geometry does not have to be so heavily oriented toward rapid cornering.

Riders with plenty of money to spend and a fondness for the ultramodern can use very expensive and unusual frame materials (such as titanium or carbon fiber) without worrying about the problems of frame whip associated with some of these. Yet at the same time, the less affluent bikie can use one of the "club racer" models such as the Gitane Tour de France or Peugeot's PX-10. These feature long wheelbases, shallow angles and considerably lower prices. And the time trial incurs little penalty for their less than gazelle-like cornering qualities.

For those with the money and the ambition, custom frame builders produce special time-trial frames, usually made of ultralight tubing such as Super Vitus or Reynolds' lighter grades, and often of lugless construction. This sort of frame requires careful work, so be prepared to spend a lot of money and wait quite a while for delivery. Most of the big-name builders overseas can make such a frame, but such US craftsmen as Al Eisentraut and Jim Redcay are just as good.

Again, however, it must be emphasized that for anything short of record attempts or really important time trials against top opponents, your high-quality road frame will do the job.

WHEELS

Ever since the wheel was invented by Eugene C. Urk in 20,000 BC, it has been the subject of much study on the part of various people. Few have been more dedicated in this pursuit than time-trial freaks. While the frame is not all that important, wheels are, and this is the place to put your money. Only when absolutely satisfied with your time-trial wheels and well supplied with top-line tires should you even consider things like the Super Vitus lugless frames.

As everyone has been told so often, rolling weight is what matters on a flat course and at constant speeds. It would appear, then, that time-trial wheels should be of the lightest construction. However, on a practical level, there is a conflict between lightness and durability. For most people, the answer will probably lie in a compromise. Obviously, it does no good to burn up the road for the first 24 miles and then have your front wheel collapse.

There is a tendency today to use rims and tires that are too light for most courses. Personally, I have noticed that those who tend to be a bit conservative in these matters seem to do better in the long run.

Riders weighing as much as 150 pounds ordinarily can use

something like the Super Champion Medaille d'Or rim (260 grams) or the roughly equivalent Mavic Extra Legere, while lightweight riders may be able to get away with something even lighter, such as Hi-E's lightest rims (212 g.). Those of us who weigh more than 150 pounds need something heavier. Probably 310 g. is a good figure for heavy riders, though many have done well with the 290-g. Fiamme Ergal rims. In fact, this last seems to be a remarkably sturdy rim for its weight and should be very suitable for time trialing over reasonably good roads.

Sealed bearing hubs are very popular in some quarters and have given good service. But many still prefer the cup-and-cone type, and certainly there's nothing smoother than a well-serviced Campagnolo Nuovo Record or Dura-Ace hub.

Some very bizarre spoke patterns turn up around time trials, but unless you're weighing less than 150 pounds (and even *that* may be pushing it) it's best to be a bit cautious. Most people will get more use out of conventional 36-spoke wheels with normal crossings. Light riders who are going to compete at national level may elect to use 32 or 28 spokes, two-cross or radial, but too many lesser riders push their luck with the same extreme setups.

Should you use high or low flange hubs? It probably doesn't matter. But if you do go in for exotic spoke setups, high flanges will help hold down the rate of spoke breakage.

TIRES

In a time trial, where no restarts are allowed, a puncture is a major disaster. While the time trial tire *should* be light, it *must* be reliable. Vulcanized cotton "cheapos" aren't even worth talking about.

For serious time trialing, high pressures are needed: 115-125 pounds, a few nervy souls going even higher. This lowers rolling resistances. In practical terms this means using silks, though there are some polyester-thread tires that seem to work very well. I have some French Dourdoignes that use a mixed silk-polyester thread; they give excellent service, take high pressures and roll out very fast.

Very light tires, such as Clement Seta Extras, weigh less than 200 g. and go down as low as 165. They are surprisingly popular, considering their fragility and whopping high price. It is true they are extremely fast tires and the logical choice for someone going for a record. As with the light wheels, however, the rider must ask whether he is really good enough to justify the expense and the risk of puncturing. The average rider will get more value out of a quality silk weighing about 230 g.

It is worth giving a little thought to the tread when buying tires for time trialing. With no real cornering involved, there is no need for a heavy tread, unless you are riding in the rain. A mat tread is fast and light, and seems to run cooler.

Whatever tires are chosen, try to keep one or two pairs for time trialing only, storing them carefully when not in use. You're asking for trouble if you ride an important time trial while using worn or repaired tires.

GEARS

Most TT courses are flat, so you don't need 10 speeds. The most popular setup among Senior men is a 13-17 cluster with a single chainring ranging from 52-54 teeth. An occasional strong man can turn a 55 or 56, particularly with the 175-mm. cranks favored by long-legged riders, but usually 53 is more realistic, or even 52. A suggested gear system for women could be 13-19, with a 50-tooth chainring. (Juniors and other younger classes must observe gear restrictions.)

In general, though, time trials are a big-gear event. Of course, one does not want to "over gear" (better a low gear you can

turn than a high one you can't). But unless you have a phenom-
enal spin, you'll have to turn big gears. Close-spaced cogs are
necessary in order to maintain a steady pace. Usually the 13-17
cluster is the norm, with different setups brought about by
changing chainwheels up front.

A few riders still time trial on a single fixed gear, usually
about a 94. The advantages are lightness, mechanical simplicity,
smoother pedal motion and the psychological value of having
only one gear and knowing it. In this case, the mind is not dis-
tracted with wondering whether to shift, nor is cadence broken
by nervous mucking about with gear changes. Theoretically
it's a sound concept, it *feels* good, and it is recommended to the
casual time trialist. But it is true that lately, no big event has
been won on a fixed gear. If there is any wind to speak of, the
optimum gear for the outbound and return legs of the run will
probably not be the same, and then too, most of us can push a
bigger gear, once rolling, than we can when starting.

BITS AND PIECES

The other components are not all that critical. Virtually any
decent derailleur will handle the close-ratio shifts involved.
Likewise, brakes are no problem, since the rider will not be using them more than twice, barring emergencies. Lightness is the
only factor that makes much difference, and even then the matter is overblown, since non-rolling weight is not as important as
rims, tires and so on.

Certainly, it is foolish to compromise safety and reliability
with such things as holes in the stem or seatpost. These jeopard-
ize one's chances of even completing the ride, and to save only a
few grams.

One reason for changing equipment, however, might be to get
a better fit. Time trialing requires that you hold a very stream-

lined position for around an hour, without fidgeting and shift-ing around. A micro-adjusting seatpost is a good investment, and it might be worthwhile to buy an adjustable stem to find out what stem extension is best for you. Such things will do much more for your times than drilling a lot of holes in your bike, and they won't make the machine any less safe, either.

Bernard Thompson

Riders using stock bikes should remove all extraneous accessories such as the water bottle and cage, the pump and its clips and the spare tire carrier. If you can't ride 25 miles without a drink of water, you aren't likely to be competitive.

A handlebar bracket for a watch is well worth the additional weight. You can then pace yourself better and avoid anxiety about how you're doing. Personally, I have found a lightweight speedometer to be worth the weight and added resistance, but I must admit this is not a popular item, except for training rides.

PERSONAL CLOTHING

The usual road racing outfit of cleated shoes, shorts and so on is the standard for time trialing as well, with one exception. A track-type jersey, smooth-finished, pocketless and close-fitting makes for less wind resistance than the usual wool road jersey. If you must use a conventional road jersey, at least pin the pockets shut: they can catch air like little drag chutes.

Some officials still allow time trialists to ride without helmets, though this is in flagrant violation of USCF rules and of common sense. Even though there is no pack riding in time trialing, crashes still occur. The time trial is a very safe form of racing, but *no* kind of cycling is so safe as to preclude the use of a helmet.

Vic Gibbons, British Best All Rounder champion in 1953-54, is a fine example of how time trialing prolongs cycling enjoyment.

Meeting
The Demands
by Lyn Lemaire

Cycling can be very physically and mentally demanding. It is not surprising, then, that followers of the sport generate a tremendous number of theories on how to best meet these demands. Most of the ideas about training have some value, but many are adhered to merely on the basis of tradition and faith. The responsibility to question alternative training methods falls upon the cyclist.

Study of the human response to physical stress is far from being an exact science, and any information concerning training effects and benefits should be approached with a critical mind.

Most of the research applying directly to the athlete is done by exercise physiologists. While the physiologist studies body systems in a normal environment, the exercise scientist studies these systems in an abnormal environment.

The body very elegantly maintains optimal, "normal" conditions for its many functions. Temperature, blood acidity, body water and blood glucose levels are just a few of the many entities that are kept in careful balance in the resting individual. When the stress of moderate or heavy exercise is placed upon the body, these entities are shaken from equilibrium.

With training, the body learns to ready its forces for the coming onslaught of the exercise bout. However, many factors will still stray from the norm, but not nearly so much as before training. This readying of forces is called a training effect. It is what the exercise physiologist studies and what the athlete attempts to maximize.

In a time trial when you begin to accelerate at the starter's signal, you are generating a form of mechanical energy. This energy is derived from contracting muscles, particularly those in your upper leg.

The molecular mechanism producing the muscle contraction is unknown, even though it has been a hotbed of research and discussion for years. Currently it is thought by some that thin, rigid, protein filaments in muscle "slide" past each other when chemical energy is released from a small compound called ATP. That is, the chemical energy stored in the ATP molecule is transformed to the mechanical energy of muscle contraction.

The chemical energy used to synthesize ATP is derived primarily from the oxidation of carbohydrates and fats. These two nutrients are broken down and then recombined with oxygen to form carbon dioxide and water. In the process a great deal of energy is released, approximately 686 calories from the complete oxidation of 180 grams (or 6.3 ounces) of glucose (the simplest carbohydrate). Some of the available energy is used to create a high energy chemical bond in ATP, and the rest is released as heat.

The biochemical pathways involved in the metabolism of foodstuffs have been well described over the last four decades. Fats are mobilized from storage in the adipose tissue and carried in the blood to the active muscle fibers. In the muscle cell the compound is completely broken down by a series of reactions that can be segregated into three stages: Beta-oxidation, the Krebs cycle and the electron-transport system.

Oxygen only enters the process in the final stage; it is an essential component of the electron transport system. Although oxygen is used only in the final stage, if the cell's supply of oxygen is inadequate all of the reactions will slow down to the point that fat is no longer mobilized from adipose tissue.

Glucose also is carried in the circulating blood. But, unlike fat, it is also stored (to some extent) in muscle tissue as glycogen. It, too, is completely disassembled by a series of biochemical reactions that can be segregated into three stages including glycolysis, the Krebs cycle and the electron-transport system. The latter two stages are the same ones involved in the breakdown of fats, and will cease to occur in the absence of oxygen.

The reactions of the first stage, glycolysis, occur regardless of the oxygen level in the cell. But the production of ATP is far less efficient. If one molecule of glucose is completely oxidized by going through the reactions of all three metabolic stages, 36 ATP molecules will be formed. If one molecule of glucose goes through only the reactions on the glygolytic pathway (and is incompletely oxidized), only two ATP will be created.

If oxygen is in short supply and only the reactions of the glycolytic pathway are active, the breakdown product will be lactic acid. For every molecule of glucose to enter the glycolytic process, two molecules of lactic acid (or lactate) will be formed. The result is an increase in the lactate concentration of both the muscle tissue and the blood, increases the acidity of both and alters the normal environment.

At rest, approximately 250 milliliters of oxygen are consumed each minute to oxidize an even proportion of fats and carbohydrates. As the exercise load increases, the relative reliance on carbohydrate as a fuel source also increases.

At workloads of greater than 70%-80% of a person's maximum aerobic capacity, the contracting muscle is largely dependent on glucose as a source of useful energy. At that power level a trained cyclist will probably be consuming between 2½ and 4 liters of oxygen each minute and will be releasing 10-20 calories each minute. Training can reduce but cannot eliminate one's reliance on glucose as an energy source.

In the initial moments of a time trial, the cell's ATP supply is quickly diminished and glucose is called upon to replenish the supply. You begin to breathe deeper and more often, heart rate increases and the amount of blood pumped increases. At the active tissue greater amounts of oxygen are extracted from the blood, and the enzymes of the metabolic pathways increase the rate of ATP, thus producing chemical reactions.

It takes a few minutes for the cardiovascular system tb catch up to the cellular demand for oxygen, and during that time the glycolytic pathway provides most of the much-needed ATP. But eventually you should reach a steady state where oxygen supply very nearly matches the demand.

Exercise physiologists have begun to study some of the variables learned and many important changes can be observed as a result of training. Controlling enzymes of glycolysis, the Krebs cycle, the electron transport system, Beta-oxidation and fat mobilization have been shown to increase in activity with training.

Glycogen stores can be increased. The numbers of protein filaments in active muscle may increase with training. The number of capillaries per muscle fiber may increase. Heart size and contractile strength increases in response to chronic overload.

The key word is stress. The body will respond to stress in a manner that tends to preserve the optimal internal environments. Chronic overload will sharpen the body's ability to cope with physical exertion, and you will feel great at being able to do things you could not do previously.

Two schools of thought seem to exist regarding the best way in which to apply the overload. One favors continuous efforts at a moderate exertion level, while the other favors intermittent bouts of near maximal effort. Working with either method as a guide will produce the training effects mentioned above, at least to some degree.

Forms of both continuous and intermittent training have been used for years. In the early part of this century, Scandanavian runners participated in interval-style training called "fartlek" or "speed play." Later some quantification was given to the method. Schedules were devised, and changes in performance were recorded as a function of the training schedule.

Interval training mixes periods of near maximal effort with periods of rest or moderate effort. Continuous training has been described recently as LSD (long, slow distance). The letters should perhaps stand for long, steady distance because this training regime calls for the output of a steady moderate effort. Runners may be able to get away with "slow" training, but a cyclist must put some speed into his rides.

The group favoring intervals would argue that the added stress of near maximal effort is necessary to achieve optimal performance and that the continuous approach does not provide the requisite stress.

Those favoring the continuous method argue that stress exists with LSD, and it is adequate providing the workout is long enough. They also argue that interval training can be too stressful, that the athlete tends to "burn out" with too many intervals.

Those in the middle suggest that training with either method will produce a training effect, and the effect will be similar if the distance covered with both techniques is the same.

Exercise physiologists have now found evidence at the biochemical level to support both groups. Muscle fibers can be classified into several overlapping categories. Most obvious is the broad grouping into red or white fibers. The former tend to contract more slowly, but they have more of the subcellular equipment for oxidizing fats and carbohydrates. They are thus much more difficult to fatigue. The white fibers are faster contracting and have less oxidative capacity. They are far easier to exhaust.

Beryl Burton, 18-time winner of the British National Women's Championships, exemplifies the effects of good training.

Bernard Thompson

LSD is probably more pleasurable than intervals, and it is a type of exercise with which every cyclist is familiar. Interval training, on the other hand, can be as unregimented as planning a course with intermittent hills or as exact as timing every on/off period to the second.

To do intervals in preparation for time trialing, the work period should be at least one minute in duration and perhaps as long as five minutes. The rest period should be defined by your pulse. Count the number of pulses in your wrist for 15 seconds, and multiply the number by four to determine your heart rate in beats per minute.

Once you have calculated your heart rate, compare it to rate which dictates that you should begin to work again. This value should fall between 60% to 70% of your maximal heart rate, predicted by subtracting your age from 220.

For example, a 30 year old might do two-minute intervals of hard work interspersed with a light work period sufficient to allow his or her heart rate to fall to between 114 and 133 beats per minute, based on a maximal predicted heart rate of 190 beats per minute.

(If you do not want to use your pulse as an indication of sufficient rest, use your own sensation of fatigue. You should feel rested enough to put a good effort into the following work period, but you should also feel somewhat out of breath. If the rest period is too long, you will be doing some sprint training instead of time trial training. Rest periods of about a minute are usually appropriate.)

The number and duration of intervals is also subjective. If five repetitions feels easy, perhaps 10 reps should have been attempted. You ought to do 2-3 more repetitions past the point of feeling tired. Most schedules should call for 4-12 repetitions and 1-3 sets (groups of repetitions).

Intervals require a great deal of mental energy as well as physical energy. For that reason alone I would advise that they not be done every day. A sample workout schedule for a week in early July is included. This is just a sample, a guideline, and it should be treated as such. A day off can be the best thing in the cyclist's training schedule, and one should certainly be taken if you are beginning to feel sluggish.

When you ride with time trialing as a goal, think about what you are doing. Think about your cadence and pace; think about your pedaling technique; think about your position on the bike. If your mind starts to wander in a time trial, your speed starts to drop.

Two things, in particular, may happen when concentration deteriorates. First, you begin to pedal less quickly and you begin to slow down. Second, you tend to sit up more. At speeds attained by most time trialists the wind, generated by both nature and your movement, is by far the greatest source of resistance. Bend your elbows and ride low in training; get used to presenting a smaller area to resisting air molecules. Then concentrate on maintaining that low position in time trial.

A word should be mentioned about weight training. Exercise scientists have espoused for years the concept of "specificity of training." In other words, if an event taxes the oxidative mechanisms of the cell, training should do the same. If an event taxes the explosive strength of the muscles involved and and their initial energy stores, training should do the same.

Because of the duration and steadiness of time trialing, it would be considered by most exercise physiologists as an "aerobic" event, one that taxes the system requiring oxygen. Weight training appears to have little effect on the athlete's oxidative potential, so one might tend to ignore it.

SAMPLE 1

Day one
40-80 miles steady

Day two
40 miles with intervals; 1 set: 8 x 1 minute ON; easy riding; 1 set: 4 x 2 minutes ON

Day three
50-80 miles, steady, moderate pace

Day four
40-50 miles; 1 set: 6 x 1½ minutes ON; easy riding; 1 set: 8 x 1 minute ON

Day five
30-60 miles; 1 set: 4 x 4 minutes ON; approx. 2 minutes OFF

Day six
rest day; rest or take a short, easy ride

Day seven
Time Trial; 10, 25, or 50 miles

SAMPLE 2

Day one
about 40 miles with intervals; 1 set: 6 x 1 minute ON, approx. 1 minute OFF; easy riding; 1 set: 4 x 3 minutes ON, approx. 2 minutes OFF

Day two
longer mileage, about 60 miles; steady riding, moderate pace

Day three
easy day; rest or short ride

Day four
30-50 miles with intervals; 2 sets: 5 x 2 minutes ON; easy riding several miles between sets

Day five
5 miles easy; 1 set: 5 x 1 minute ON; complete 50 miles at moderate, steady pace

Day six
50 miles with a group in a pace line

Day seven
Time Trial; 10, 25, or 50 miles

Eliminating Human Error

by Cy and Marge Campbell

Dave Hendrick may miss an occasional time trial in San Diego, but his timer will be there.

Dave has combined his lifetime interest in electronics with his love of cycling to develop a unique dual time recorder that virtually does away with human error.

A bulky wooden box complete with a silver case atop it and two metal strips, are regular features at San Diego, Calif., Wheelmen time trials. And no conscientious timekeeper would dare trust his own computation without it.

When the Wheelmen originally began the East County Time Trials in 1970, a primitive sports car rally stopwatch was used to time the riders. Despite all the care, errors of as much as a minute were common, particularly when new members or bystanders were pressed into service. Even a new stopwatch with a split-second hand failed. Riders who strove mightily to beat their own previous records were faced with being "good sports" and accepting erroneous results although they were sure the timer had erred.

Dave wanted to ride almost as much as he wanted the results to be accurate. He watched the market for every gadget that could be used. When a small electronic digital stopwatch that could be read in bright sunlight appeared, he bought it. With this, the timer could simply press a button without taking his eyes off the rider as he crossed the finish line. The watch would stop immediately, and the score could be recorded.

As soon as the button was pushed again, the indicator flipped on to catch up to the correct time, ready to record the next cyclists' time.

But Dave was still not satisfied. When two riders crossed the finish line within a second or two, frequently the second time had to be judged, rather than accurately recorded.

Glen Graves

Dave was concerned with this dependence on a timekeeper's constant attention. How much better it would be if the rider himself tripped the mechanism as he rode across the finish line. Dave took the problem to his drawing board and experimented for six months.

From this his first invention evolved—the Quartz Accutron, an electronic digital timer. It used a metal strip, a timing plate, placed on the road. When a rider's front wheel went over it, the timer's latch circuit froze the display down to 1/100th of a second. After the time was recorded, the timer was reset automatically to the correct elapsed time.

As Dave explained it, "Official races use an electric eye device, but we can't because cars passing would complicate our recordings."

Unfortunately, about 10% of the riders, for one reason or another, failed to cross the strip. The timer pressed a small button himself to stop the time.

But there were still problems. The timekeepers complained that fairly often two or more riders came by with only fractions of a second between them. They couldn't record the time and reset the button fast enough. What could Dave do to help?

After 18 months, Dave developed the Alpha 4000 Bike Timer.

In this, two displays are used, timing each to 1/100th of a second. They are connected to some 80 integrated circuits that can freeze at two different times. Two metal road strips are placed about five feet apart, to catch two riders coming across as though in a pacer line. And with a hand set as a backup, a third rider's time is also recorded accurately. The Alpha 4000 also contains a computing circuit to subtract the start from finish time and come up with an elapsed time.

You'd think that would be the epitome of success. But Dave wasn't satisfied with the human element in the countdown for take off. Some of us, by nature, are more slowly geared than others, and when seconds are precious, no one wants to have his time dependent upon a drawling timer.

The Alpha 4000 has a built-in audio countdown circuit. Five low-tone beeps, followed by a higher beep, signal "Go." With the intervals of starting times established on the front panel, the times are locked in and cannot be changed.

Of course, when Dave became Time Trial chairman, he rechecked the length of the course with his own special device. He insists, with great modesty, that this device is in no way as accurate as a surveyor with a chain, but the riders who are aware of Dave's insistence upon detail and conforming to the established rules, are well content with his judgments. Cottonwood Course, found to be 11.6 miles long, was shortened to an exact 10 miles.

This year, a 25-mile course was developed, beginning near Southwestern College in Bonita, Calif. Recognizing Dave's ability and realizing how accurate his equipment is, the Southern California District asked if their 25-Mile Time Trials could be run on this new course. (Riders who were successful in this competition qualified to compete in the Nationals.)

Dave soon decided to devote even his working hours to the bicycle world. He has opened up Dave's Bike Shop at 7761 University Avenue in La Mesa, Calif. When he turned in his formal resignation to Khrondel, manufacturers of drag strip time equipment, they told him they were interested in putting together a circuit board that would make assembling other dual time recorders easier for him. If you think your own time trials would be improved with Dave's equipment why not write and ask him about it.

Allowing Concentration Some Time by Simon Leigh

Pain, so they say, is only a state of mind. Right. But it's a very painful state of mind, as every time-trialer rediscovers in that horrible first mile. Your body may be fit, strong and warmed-up, but once you bend it double and start cranking those metal blocks round and round, it never quite *believes* it.

But pain itself is not the problem. Pain can't stop you, unless it's new, strange and generating panic. Pure pain (unamplified by fear) is horrible, but bearable. After all, as Steve Woznick confesses, in a kilometer "the last 200 meters is murder, . . . the physical pain is like you're bloated . . . (but) it's that day and it's who wants it most." Besides, pure pain, unlike fear, anger and the humiliation of defeat, is wonderfully forgettable. After the race you can't even remember it clearly.

The problem of pain is that it undermines your concentration. Each time your concentration lapses, pain craftily slows down your body. Enter mental pain, and determination to get lost seconds back, by speeding up. But the problem here is that weary bodies hate being disturbed. The pain of increasing the effort always seems to outweigh the relief of decreasing it. So, in theory, to minimize the pain you should ride the whole time trial at a constant effort, some constant percentage of your maximum.

Your maximum is always higher than you think. Prove it to yourself in training. On a flat road, ride a mile in, say 78 inches at a constant 100 rpm, then switch to 83 inches. It hurts, but as soon as your body realizes that you mean it, the pain starts to fade.

Sure, there's a limit, but that initial change-of-load pain will stop many riders from even approaching their limit. *If* you could push a constant 100 rpm in 100-inch gear, you'd be well under Alf Enger's world record time for the 25-mile time trial and pressing him for first to break the 50-minute barrier.

Once your body stabilizes at the high-power output, it can keep going, with proper fueling, for quite a while, which is why the average speed for 30- and 50-mile TTs is surprisingly close to that for 25s. The problem with this constant-effort plan is that people, being human, don't relish the idea of constant suffering for the eternity it takes to get to the finish.

Failing these arrangements, the lonely time trialer can best adopt the "moving finish line" mental approach. Go hard to that road sign, then (*that* pain forgotten instantly) hold the pace until that tree, until the top of this little hill (you can rest on the way down), change up and go *hard* down the hill, keep that gear on the flat. If you've timed it right, you burn out your last shreds of energy to reach the real finish line. No possibility of a finishing sprint, for if you can, you've been slacking off. If you can mount your bike to ride home afterwards, you've been slacking off. The quickest time trialer I ever saw finish couldn't even get *off* his bike.

Very few athletes can push themselves to total exhaustion, and just as well. The body's endocrine system doesn't like being blown apart too often.

Exceptional motivation, coupled with pedaling skill, power output and endurance can break records. But do the ace riders also have some hidden weapon in their ability to handle pain? To claim that they "like to suffer" makes little sense. A true masochist would ride a time trial on half-inflated tires, or stop just before the finish for a hot dog. Do the greats feel less pain, or put up with more?

Eddie Merckx recently broke the world 30-minute ergometer record in Cologne with a ride of 450 watts, the machine's maximum. Most other world-class athletes, especially runners (who admittedly lack Eddie's pedaling efficiency) finish the test exhausted, with a lactic acid reading of around 20.0. Eddie's reading was 4.0 and he wasn't even badly winded, but he was in pain. How well does he cope?

My hunch is that the top riders are unusually good at blocking out their pain, so they *feel* less. Perhaps if you start with high pain tolerance plus high motivation, you can train yourself to handle high pain loads without losing your spin.

My hunch is that the dedicated time trialer can, through hard training and competition, increase his ability to produce hormones that dull the pain of muscle fatigue, and enable the body to work closer to its maximum power output.

Familiarity with pain breeds contempt, so you can learn to register that initial burst of pain as mere "lactic acid buildup and oxygen debt." Your body will catch up with it by the second or third mile. Grind away—then at 45 minutes or so, when you start worrying you're going to die, you'll register the pain as mere bodily adjustments during the switch-over from the glucose-burning system to the much more efficient (though somewhat less powerful) fat-burning mode. Press on regardless, through the wall. Cramps? With proper nutrition and fueling, you won't get them.

THE RECIPE

Directions
On the Official Road by Jim Harper

Almost every racing club uses time trials as part of a training program. A club time trial gives both club coaches and individual riders a yardstick to measure training progress and helps evaluate various training programs. Clubs use various lengths of courses for these events but they all have one thing in common: straight roads with few or no intersections.

Another form of time trials is the hill climb. It's an individual effort against the clock, up a hill. Riders are sent up the hill at one-minute intervals in the same manner as the road time trial.

Racing clubs always are on the lookout for flat, straight roads on which to run individual road time trials. The reason is that flat roads produce faster times and fast times are a requirement to qualify for the US Cycling Federation's National Time Trial Championships. The USCF has 49 districts and each district conducts a district championship to qualify riders for the Nationals. Most districts will stage their championships during a mid-June weekend this year to qualify riders for the Nationals in Seattle, Wash., in late July.

Naturally, each district will be looking for the flattest, straightest, safest course on which to run its championships. This district championship qualifying course must measure 25 miles.

In all fairness, it should be pointed out that any time riders start at the same point and finish at the same point, this would be a fair and legitimate time trial regardless of the type or length of the course. However, when it comes to picking a course for the district championships, it must be flat and fast to qualify riders for the Nationals.

Maybe the riders in your club would be interested in riding time trials if you found a course for them. Here is what to look for when picking a safe, fast 25-mile time trial course.

STRAIGHT AND FLAT FOR 13 MILES

The single most important thing to look for is a straight, flat road. The road should measure 13 miles on the odometer if you expect it to measure out 12½ miles. You must avoid turns because they create the danger of head-on collisions between cyclists or even worse, between cyclists and cars. All turns require marshalls, one reason to avoid them, and bends also should be avoided. If a rider can "shorten" the course by crossing the center of the road, then that bend has too great an angle. A bend such as this would also require an official to keep the riders "honest." In a time trial, a contestant may never cross the center of the road, even at a 90-degree turn.

NO INTERSECTIONS

All intersections create a safety hazard in a time trial. Intersections also require marshalls, and manpower is always in short supply (especially during inclement weather, when it is needed the most). Don't pick a course with a traffic light because it gives riders who "make" the light too great of an advantage over others who get "caught" by the light. Stop signs on the course present similar problems.

A GOOD SURFACE

Check the road surface by riding the course on your bike. On the bike, you will be checking the right-hand side of the road where the contestant will ride. This is the important area, not the center of the road. A good surface allows a time trial rider to use lighter wheels and tires. Needless to say, roads crossing railroad tracks should be avoided.

SHELTER FROM THE WIND

Crosswinds and head winds can cause havoc with good times in a time trial. Winds also can blow to a rider's advantage. A

A sign is an invaluable safety aid to time trialists.

Harry Esterly

rider may start early with no appreciable wind blowing, another rider may start an hour later into a stiff head wind. This same head wind would be acting as a tail wind for the rider who started an hour earlier. So try to pick a course with trees on each side of the road or pick a road located in a valley.

NO MORE THAN LIGHT VEHICULAR TRAFFIC

The sport of time trials was developed so bicycle riders could compete on the roads shared by vehicular traffic. However, in the interest of safety, try to choose a course that has light traffic. Riders also must recognize that a time trial is not run on closed roads and vehicular interference is an unfortunate possibility. Riders must respect the right of the motorist, obey traffic laws and ride on the right-hand side of the road.

You finally have located a course that meets most of the

aforementioned standards. The next step is to decide at which ends the start-finish and the turnaround should be.

The turn is most important. Try to pick a portion of the road with extra width on the right-hand side. This will allow the rider to swing wide and make the turn at higher speed. The traffic cone you use to mark the turnaround is always placed on the center line of the road. Make sure the road is flat in the turning area. Pick a spot without a high crown in the center as this will lessen the chances of spills on the turns.

A course is always measured from the turn to the start-finish. To measure a course, you need a can of spray paint, pencil, pad and walking wheel. These wheels are also called estimating or measuring wheels. Fence builders and paving contractors use them to estimate distances.

The wheels come in two sizes, 15½ and 23 inches, with mechanical foot counters. The wheel manufacturer says the 15½-inch wheel is accurate to within 18 inches in one mile and the 23-inch wheel is accurate to within 12 inches in one mile.

The wheels cost approximately $90 and may be purchased from Rolotape, 1301 Olympic Boulevard, Santa Monica, Calif.

Cones are used to mark the turnaround because they are made of pliable plastic. If a rider falls on one at the turn, he won't be hurt by the cone. Don't ask a marshall to stand in the middle of the road and have the riders go around him. When two riders are going through the turn at the same time, the marshall may move to avoid one rider and inadvertently interfere with the next rider.

Start off by painting a "plus" at the spot you will place your traffic cone. The mark should be on the center line. Your measurement will start there and continue on the center line or traffic line in the road. If you picked a road without a painted line, your chances of measuring accurately are very slim. The wheel must be rolled in a straight line, with no wobble, to be as accurate as possible.

After you have measured 5280 feet, put a small paint line on the road, made a note in your book about your location, reset your foot counter and start again. Repeat this procedure to the 12-mile mark.

Now look at the left side of the road (facing the turn) and ask yourself, "Would this be a good finishing spot? Is there enough room for a timekeeper and a recorder? Would the time-keeper have a good view up the road?"

If the answer is "yes," keep it in mind and measure out 2640 feet and put another paint marker at 12½ miles. Now measure out another 2640 feet and put down your last paint mark. Now consider the three points. Would the 12-mile mark make a good finish or would the 13-mile mark make a good start?

The reason for the marks at 12, 12½ and 13 miles is to aid in separating the start and finish line. If you were going to run a small time trial with 50 riders or less, there wouldn't be much need to separate the start and finish.

If you run a time trial with more than 50 entries, however, you can't have two or three riders sprinting for the same line on which you are starting another rider. The starting rider can't hear the starting timekeeper's countdown with people cheering for the finishing riders. The start and finish are always separated at a major time trial.

It's a good idea to start off by separating your start and fin-ish. It's too late to change when you have more entries than you expected. If you choose to separate the start-finish by one mile, you would start at the 13-mile mark and finish at the 12. This layout makes the course easy to mark.

Painting the "miles to go" with spray paint on the right side of the road eliminates the need for various signs on the course. However, if these signs are available, they should be used.

Another way to separate the start-finish line is to measure 200 yards with a steel tape from the 12½-mile mark toward the turn. Make that the finish. Measure 200 yards in the other direction from the 12½-mile mark and make that your start. Now you have the start and finish separated by 400 yards.

A course should be marked well with signs. The signs going out should read, "turn, one mile," "turn, 200 meters." The signs on the return should read, "one mile" and "200 meters." A large board with black and white squares should mark the finish along with tape on the road. The riders should be able to see the finish sign on the way "out."

I have just explained the minimum requirements for a club 15-mile time trial course. The next step is to have the course measurement certified. A course can be certified by having it measured by a licensed surveyor. A certified 25-mile time trial course should be the goal of every USCF district in 1977.

The cost to measure a 13-mile course with a one-way center line measurement should be less than $200. It will take one licensed surveyor and two helpers six hours to measure the 13-mile course (with a steel tape) at a cost of $30 per hour. The records committee will accept a one-way measurement on a straight road.

If the road has a curve that will allow a rider to "shorten" the course by crossing the center line, a measurement along each side of the road would be required. This may run the cost to about $400 for certification. Never sacrifice a straight road for another with a curve just because it is more conveniently located, or has parking facilities. The need for the straight, flat road can't be emphasized enough.

The difference in elevation between the start and finish

must be within one foot and the start-finish can't be separated by more than one mile. Area clubs could share the cost of certification.

Two more signs should be added to your collection of time trial signs. They should be big: about five feet high and three feet wide. They should read, "Caution, bicycle riders on road next 13 miles." One should be placed about 150 yards before the start. These signs will alert motorists that a cycling activity is taking place before they motor up to your starting line at high speed.

The safety of time trials is one of the most attractive aspects of the sport. People who have taken to the bicycle as a source of better physical conditioning soon start looking for some way to measure their progress. Veterans, who no longer find appealing the banging of shoulders in high-speed turns, are switching to this event.

Every organizer or promoter of every time trial should make every effort to conduct the event as safely as possible, on an accurately measured course with proper timing equipment. Our sport will grow in stature only after we, the promoters of time trials, attain that degree of professionalism this event so richly deserves.

USCF Time Trial Rules

Because of the nature and size of time trials today, organizers and directors must adhere to a strict set of rules so the racing will continue as smoothly as possible. The United States Cycling Federation (USCF) recognizes the need for order at the trials and has developed strict rules governing the supervision of and participation in time trials.

What is presented here is a condensation of the rules established by the USCF. These are to acquaint cyclists with the atmosphere and execution of time trials and do not represent the official language of the rules established by the USCF.

THE START

● All riders will start the trial in a numerical sequence as stated on a start sheet. The start sheet will be published before the start of the trials and shall be available for riders' perusal before the start of the time trials. Those riders not appearing on the start sheet shall not be allowed to start.

● A rider's time will start when he or she is scheduled to start and if a rider starts later than his appointed time (recorded on the start sheet), his appointed time will be used to establish his timing. Starts in an individual time trial shall be at one-minute intervals. Starts in a two-man team time trial should be at two-minute intervals. Starts in four-man team time trials should be at three- or four-minute intervals.

● Riders arriving late for a start may only start with the starter's permission and may not, in any way, interfere with the starting of other riders scheduled to follow.

● Riders shall be held by an official at the start, but shall not be restrained or pushed. A rider starting before the signal is subject to disqualification.

● No restarts will be allowed for any rider suffering a mechanical breakdown or a flat tire immediately prior to or immediately after the start.

ETIQUETTE AND SAFETY

● Riders must ride on the right side of the right-hand lane, except to pass. Any rider who crosses the center line of the road, or crosses to the left lane, will be disqualified. Riders must stay in the right-hand lane of a road with two or more lanes.

● Riders must pass to the left of the rider being passed. The passing rider will move to the left when he or she is 80 feet (25 meters) from the rider ahead, and not return to the right side of the road until well clear of the other rider. When a passing cyclist draws abreast of the rider being passed, the rider being passed will allow the passing cyclist to pass clearly. The rider being passed shall not take pace or shelter behind the passing cyclist.

● Any rider found to be drafting another rider is subject to disqualification. No warning need be given by an official.

● Riders should look where they are going and not ride with their heads down.

COURSE AND EQUIPMENT

● The responsibility of keeping on the correct course rests with the rider. A rider must go around the traffic cone or object marking the turn-around point.

● No rider shall have a following vehicle and no rider may take pace from or draft a vehicle. If any vehicle belonging to a parent, friend or teammate is found on the course while the time trial is in progress, the rider will be subject to disqualification.

● A rider may not file a protest if a vehicle inadvertently

interferes with his or her progress. Riders must recognize that a road time trial is not run on a closed course, and vehicular interference or a train crossing is an unfortunate possibility.

● Road bicycles shall be used. Track bicycles with a front hand brake and fixed wheel may be used for an individual time trial.

THE FINISH

● After a rider crosses the finish line, he or she should not go back to ask the timekeeper for a finishing time until the event is finished.

● All times will be recorded to the nearest second. They will be recorded by hour:minute:second. For record purposes, three watches are required (one electrical) and time recorded to one hundredth of a second.

● The second rider's time will be recorded as the elapsed time in a two-man team trial. The third rider's time will be recorded in a four-man team trial.

USCF District Representatives

NORTHEAST

Name	Address	City, State, Zip
G.S. Jones	24 Brown Ave.	Lundenburg, Mass. 01462
A. McKown	37 Water St.	Exeter, N.H. 03833
L.J. Poulin	558 Riverside Dr.	Augusta, Me. 04330
W.R. Cram	Box 272	Dorset, Vt. 05251
J.R. Tosi Sr.	5 Prospect Hill Terr.	Warehouse Pt., Conn. 06088
V.F. Menci	1 Hunterdon St.	Somerville, N.J. 08876
H. Seubert	67 Birchwood Dr.	New Hyde Park, N.Y. 11040
D. Houser	11049 Riverview Dr.	Hadley, N.Y. 12835
C.E. Hendricks	331 South Creek Dr.	Depew, N.Y. 14043
B. Smith	38-40 W. Oakland Ave.	Doylestown, Pa. 18901
G. Sandruck	1719 Pin Oak Rd.	Baltimore, Md. 21234

SOUTHEAST

Name	Address	City, State, Zip
G.M. Teeuwen	946 Shillelagh Rd.	Chesapeake, Va. 23323
C. Messer	202 Ballengee St.	Hinton, W. Va. 25951
H. Mills	1201 W. Fifth Ave.	Lexington, N.C. 27292
F.A. Graham	4044 Springhill Rd.	Columbia, S.C. 29204
M. Fitzgerald	1067 Ocean Blvd.	St. Simons Isld., Ga. 31522
C. de Block	6260 SW Eighth St.	N. Lauderdale, Fla. 33068
T. Carlisle	3317 Mountainside Rd.	Birmingham, Ala. 35243
H. Horn	2110 Chillicothe	Knoxville, Tenn. 37921
L. Savell	205 Virginia	Indianola, Miss. 38751
B. Zeman	2120 Woodford Pl.	Louisville, Ky. 40205
G. McKenzie	1270A Laurel St.	Baton Rouge, La. 70802
M. Widder	Carlson Terr. V-207	Fayetteville, Ark. 72701

MIDWEST

Name	Address	City, State, Zip
G. Weyrick	Box 6343	Akron, Ohio 44312
B. Arnold	10580 Johnson Rd.	Fort Wayne, Ind. 46808
D. Croft	15 Elm Park Blvd.	Pleasant Ridge, Mich. 48069
K. Jury	1424 Burnett	Ames, Iowa 50010
V. Pearce	1109 W. Birch Ave.	Milwaukee, Wis. 53209

P. Voxland	2217 23rd Ave. South	Minneapolis, Minn. 55404
Dr. E. Scholz	1128 N. Seventh St.	Fargo, N.D. 58102
A. Herreweyers	4836 N. Melvina St.	Chicago, Ill. 60630
H. Althoff	Box 15102	St. Louis, Mo. 63110
G. War Wee	1029 Tennessee No. 2	Lawrence, Kan. 66044
J. Blackwell	3105 S. 106th St.	Omaha, Neb. 68124

SOUTHWEST

Name	Address	City, State, Zip
K.R. Driessel	Box 591	Tulsa, Okla. 74102
C. Livingston	912 Overhill	Bedford, Tex. 76021
E.T. Nesdill	5040 E. Sheridan St.	Phoenix, Ariz. 85008
G. Gamble	11444 Freeway Pl. NE	Albuquerque, N.M. 87123

ROCKY MOUNTAINS

Name	Address	City, State, Zip
E.W. Anacker	1905 W. College	Bozeman, Mont. 59715
R.E. Knodel	507 4-J Road	Gillette, Wyo. 82716
H. van Soolen	3622 South 4840 W.	Hunter, Utah 84102
S. Rautus	1590 Xavier No. 301	Denver, Colo. 80204

WEST

Name	Address	City, State, Zip
R.W. Enright	612 S. Dunsmuir Ave.	Los Angeles, Calif. 90036
K. Parso	500 W. Santa Maria, 130	Santa Paula, Calif. 93060
R. Garner	2755 El Camino	Redwood City, Calif. 94063
A. Kovner	28 Oneawa St., Kailua	Honolulu, Hawaii 96734
E. Drapela	1320 Corum Ave.	Eugene, Ore. 97401
B. Kaye	Box 33	Black Diamond, Wash. 98010
E. Zeitler	2108 Alston Rd.	Fairbanks, Alaska 99701

Something New in Time Trials
by John Wilcockson

Time trialing is a traditional sport, but it has undergone more major changes in the past decade than in its previous 70 years. New technology, new ideas giving rise to many different types of time trials and the universal spread of the automobile have irreversibly altered the sport.

Accurate timing is an essential factor in time trialing, but only recently has it benefited from modern technology. In fact, the Road Time Trials Council (RTTC) of England has accepted only this year that events under their control can be timed by electronic timers.

The majority of time trials are still timed by traditional means—hand-held watches. But the day is coming when electronics take over completely. Olympic track races now are fully electronic, and the Union Cyclists Internationale (UCI) will not accept short-distance records not recorded by electronic timers.

Just as timing methods have improved, so have times. Smoother road surfaces and modern training techniques have contributed largely to this, but the main reason has been the dramatic acceleration in bicycle technology.

When I began time trialing about 15 years ago, the majority of riders had just one bike (which they used for touring as well as for racing). The frame was of standard 72-degree parallel angles, with enough clearance for fenders. It was not ideal for any of its different uses, but it was serviceable.

The next development, in the late '60s, was the multi-purpose racing bike that could be used for criteriums as well as time trials. Angles of the frame increased to 73 degrees parallel, clearances were reduced and, under the influence of Eddy Merckx, equipment was drilled.

At the same time, gear sizes got bigger and bigger, until some time trialists were seen struggling with giant chainwheels (perhaps with 58 teeth) and tiny sprockets (as small as 12 teeth) on bikes made dangerously flimsy by drilling. The result was an unsightly riding style that rarely brought about any great improvement in standards.

This drill-everything era has not passed completely, but today's time trialist is more likely to use a machine built especially for the job. More sophisticated technology—in metallurgy as well as bicycle design—has given rise to the special time trial bike.

The record-breaking racer must use high gears to compete at the top. World Champion Freddy Maertens currently favors a high of 55 x 13 (or 114.2 inches). To pedal such a gear effectively, it is necessary to sit over the bottom bracket and so the frame should have a seat angle as steep as 75 degrees.

Big gears, when used correctly, put higher stresses on the frame tubes. Therefore, lightness is now obtained by using lightweight tubing such as Reynolds 753, special lightweight 531 or ultra-light Columbus. Rigidity is the key word, so most of the drilled accessories also have disappeared, only to be replaced by equipment that incorporates titanium and carbon alloy parts.

NEW IDEAS

Time trialing has diversified considerably since early 1960. Before then, it was almost unknown for an open time trial to be less than 25 miles in length, and time trial stages in top races (such as the Tour de France) were normally of 50 kilometers or more.

Team time trials were in their infancy and the prologue time trial still had to be invented. Today, the team event is one of the most popular world championship events and there is hardly a single stage race that doesn't include a short, individual time trial.

The US Time Trial Team competed at the 1970 Worlds.

Bernard Thompson

One hundred kilometers is the length of four-up team time trials at the world championships.

There are signs that an individual road time trial may be included in the world championships also. At the last UCI congress in Geneva, the Union's president stated that the world professional championship should be decided over a series of races—including an individual time trial.

Change also has taken place in recent years to the Gran Prix des Nations—the leading time trial promotion in the world. In its first 40 years of history, the Nations was always held in the Paris region, usually over a distance of between 100-140 kilometers.

In 1973, the event moved to the west of France, mainly because of difficulties with heavy motor traffic near Paris.

Another difference in the Nations is the opening up of the event to both amateurs and professionals—perhaps a pointer of how sport as a whole is developing.

Whatever that future may be, there will remain a firm place in the time trial calendar for long-distance events that are now proving more popular with tourists than with pure racers. It is certain that professionals never will be attracted by time trialing of the long distances demanded in events such as the 12 hours of Gland in Switzerland and the Onondaga Cycling Club's 24-hour event in New York state.

These long-distance tests are a challenge to the cyclist who wants to give his body and bike a greater test than the standard century or double century tourist rides. This is not the case in England, though, where 12s and 24s always have been seriously contested.

However, the records for both those events were set eight years ago, and during the '70s there has been a marked reduction in the support of long-distance time trials. One of the four annual 24-hour time trials has disappeared from the British calendar, and much discussion has centered on whether the 12-hour should be cut from the qualifying events for the prestigious British Best All Rounder (BBAR) competition. The future of long-distance time trials is likely to be a compromise between the demands of time trialists and the wishes of tourists who want accuracy and organization.

Returning to short-distance time trials, the emergence of pro-logues in stage racing cannot be overemphasized. They are events that add prestige to a top promotion, as well as giving immediate time differences in the race standings. Before their introduction, there was little to see by crowds at the starting town of a race like the Tour de France. Now, they can watch (at close quarters) every competitor in the race as he fights for seconds in a lone effort lasting 5-10 minutes.

With judicious placing of the best riders at the end of the starting list, an organizer can give the spectators an exciting climax to this "race within the race." Tension can be height-ened by staging the prologue time trial on a tight circuit in a city center.

An event that could well emerge in the next decade is the medium-gear time trial. This is normally a 25-mile race in which riders are limited to using a maximum gear of 72 inches. This could be either a fixed wheel on a track bike, or a "screwed down" derailleur machine.

Such time trials were very popular in England up until the early 1960s, with up to 30 medium-gear 25s being held in the month of March. (The record for a "25" ridden on a 72-in. fixed wheel stands at just over 59 minutes—equivalent to a cadence of 117 rpm.)

These limited-gear events, perhaps staged at 10 miles, could assist novice time trialists in learning the basic art of pedaling. This is particularly important with school-age and women cy-clists, who often are tempted to push big gears because they have read that "this is how Merckx wins time trials."

THE CAR AND TIME TRIALS

No one factor has had more influence on the recent evolu-tion of time trialing than the increased number of automobiles. The trend has produced both good and bad side effects.

Some argue that divided highways and smoother pavements have benefited the sport by making it easier to record fast times (particularly at 10, 25 and 50 miles), while others say that the increased volume and speed of motor traffic has made time trialing too dangerous. The real answer may lie somewhere between these two views.

In England, there are very few courses that do not incorporate long stretches of divided highway. This has given rise to the term "dragstrip," because competitors using such roads are helped considerably by the slipstream of passing cars and trucks. This has enabled time trialists to use very high gears.

There has been much controversy in British time trialing circles about "motor assisted" time trialists, giving rise to the appearance of official RTTC observers to make spot checks.

A two-up TT on an isolated road precludes auto dangers.

Bernard Thompson

The slipstream effect is sometimes accentuated by a rider's helper driving a car behind him at a steady, slow speed, thus ensuring that a steady stream of passing vehicles will be "delivered" to the rider.

Such motor-related problems can be solved by introducing more stringent rules, but it will become increasingly more difficult to find quiet highways on which to promote time trials. Where freeways are built, the old highway often is neglected by the authorities. The pavement deteriorates, making it unsuitable for bike racing.

The answer could be to use freeway-type roads, but at an hour when motor traffic is negligible. This could bring time trialing back to its origins, when events started at dawn and finished before most people were eating breakfast.

This method would satisfy the requirements of riders and officials seeking fair and equal conditions for time trialing, but would hardly meet the demands of events that seek publicity. Therefore, more important events are likely to be held on courses and circuits that utilize quieter, but hillier, back roads.

Such courses already are becoming popular, particularly in England, where flat, main road courses have been the goal of time trialing promoters. There are now many hilly time trials promoted every weekend throughout the racing season. This is another trend that US clubs could copy, because these time trials teach competitors to be more aggressive than on a straight, out-and-back course.

Perhaps the greatest benefit of the motor age has been the increased mobility of everyone, so that cyclists can travel hundreds of miles to compete in an event. This can increase standards by bringing together the top time trialists more frequently, but it can also mean less support for local events which would need both local and outside publicity.

A BRIGHT FUTURE

From this review of time trialing, it can be seen that its image has altered drastically in the past decade, and not always for the better. But my overall conclusion is that there is a bright future for this traditional branch of cycle sport.

Getting
Down to Specifics
by Simon Leigh

Your legs are screeching but you only hear that tune in your head that keeps cranking you along at 110 rpm. You're *flying*, propelled by the terror of slowing and wasting all that work you've put in so far. This will be your quickest 25 ever.

Your silk jersey is soaked. Oh, no! Exxon truck ahead, thundering toward you. As it passes you drop your head and pump everything into your legs. The air wave hits and you keep grinding away, keeping up that cadence—once it drops you'll never get it back. Hang on for a few more yards . . . you're in the clear again.

The finish lies just a mile ahead but you're *dying*. You've left it all on the road. Oh no—another truck! You peep under your left armpit and see your savior upside-down in the shape of a Winnebago, Go! with nothing behind it! Go! Pull out, Go! Go! . . .

You finish, and the pain slides down into your legs. Your time is good, your best, excellent.

And somebody just beat you by two seconds . . . .

What can you do? That evening you find yourself peering at your bike looking for places to file off another half-ounce: those ornamental spikes on the mounting bands of your Campy front derailleur and levers, for instance? Or how about going whole hog and buying that titanium frameset?

A more fruitful—and less expensive—approach is to set up your road racing bike to reduce air drag to an absolute minimum. As Jack Lambie's figures show, at 30 m.p.h., 86% of your total leg power goes into overcoming air drag ("Catch the Wind," *Bike World*, Oct. 1974).

Bicycle lightening programs are fashionable status games, fun to play if you've got a spare $100. A pound saved on a 22-pound bike feels great. But once you're aboard, if you weigh, say, 170 lbs., it's really only a 0.5% gain. And it won't cut 0.5% off your total time, either. In a flat TT, you're only accelerating your mass for a half minute or so, at the start and after the U-turn. The rest of the time is just legs.

"But every little gram helps." Sure, but less than you'd think. At 30 m.p.h. on the flat, a 0.5% weight reduction will reduce your total energy requirement by 0.5% times 0.006 (the rolling resistance figure for bicycles) times 30 (m.p.h.) over 375; or, 0.0000024 horsepower. Compared with your total energy requirement at 30 m.p.h. (no wind) quoted by Lambie as 0.714 horsepower, that's a gain of—wait for it—0.0003 per cent. Hmmm . . . .

So squat down in front of your bike and take an air mole-cule's-eye view. To cut your TT time significantly you've got to cut an 86% air drag figure, even if it means a weight penalty. One fourth of your total air drag is from your bicycle itself (Cranfield Institute of Technology report no. 106). Let's start there.

SETTING UP YOUR BIKE
• *Pump.* A carbon dioxide Tire-Flator in the back pocket makes better sense than a pump. But if you have to carry one, mount it flat, under the top tube.

• *Pedals.* The front face of each pedal pushes against the slipstream on every stroke. The new, super-light Phil Wood pedals present an outrageous six square inches of solid surface. Buy those trick Cinelli Sprint 71 pedals which clamp directly onto the special cleat. They present about as much drag as a bare axle. (Plus a thin-soled pair of shoes just for TTs).

If you're feeling creative and want to grind half the metal off the lower front face of a road pedal, start with a steel one, steel being stronger than alloy. (Air drag first, weight second—it's a whole new way of evaluating components.)

● *Gears.* For flattish TTs with predictable winds, ride a fixed gear and change your gear just before the start. Gear for the windward leg, and spin like mad on the leeward. If you only need two gears, build up a two-sprocket freewheel. Screw the derailleur adjuster stops right in, and feel proud—you just fabricated a no-cost two-speed Positron.

● *Front Derailleur.* Because their workings are tucked in behind the seat tube, the Campy Valentino Extra and the plastic Simplex are best.

Slacken the cable so that in high ratio the lever is horizontal instead of straight up. If you don't need the gear range, remove the front derailleur, lever, cable and guide (use a five-speed guide), and one chainwheel.

● *Rear Derailleur.* For frontal area, Campy and its copies look good. But Dura Ace and the Suntour Cyclone look a shade better.

It's fashionable to drill out the changer lever, but filing it to half width would be a lot easier. You can grind off the stop and let the lever point horizontally forward in top gear.

The bolt holding the lever assembly (under the down tube) has got to go. Ideally, you should braze the assembly on (and braze the cable guides, waterbottle supports and pump pegs while you're at it). Or switch to the new Suntour Cyclone levers, which are smooth underneath.

Handlebar controls are a drag—all that extra cable plus the two levers hanging down like spoilers in the slipstream. But if you adjust them to lie horizontal while you are in your TT gear, and use minimum-length cables in Ultra-Glide housings, they're superb.

● *Brakes.* Centerpulls, especially the cheap, short-armed ones, have less air drag than side pulls. This is because they have less cable, and do not have four great arms sticking out in the wind. Remove that quick-release hardware, the wheel guides, the brake adjuster assembly and the rubber hoods on the levers. To be really slick, remove those big road racing levers altogether and braze on a skinny all-steel lever from a kid's bike. You only brake once during a TT.

And mount your special TT brake pads, half-worn and tapered to a point at the front, with the mounting rod ends sawed off flush so they don't stick out.

But if all this seems too much trouble just to gain 30 seconds or so, at least take a firm grip on the quick release tab of your front Mafac. Twist, so it faces sideways instead of directly into the slipstream.

To reduce cable air drag, bend those Ultra-Glide cables sharply and tape them along the rear of the handlebars. Snip off any protruding wire cables.

● *Fork ends.* Why pedal four flat-fronted fork ends through the air? Round off the face of the front forks, then take a thoughtful look at that left rear one. Does that inch or so of spare metal on the bottom really *do* anything? Hacksaw it off and round the front edge.

● *Quick-release levers* (Campy). Put the rear lever on the freewheel side, pointing down in front of the derailleur. This will open up the air a little before it hits that chunky derailleur. For the same reason, put the front lever on the right (chainwheel) side, pointing ahead and downward at 45 degrees.

On the other end of the spindles, place the wire loops vertical to and ahead of the hub. File off any protruding spindle threads.

● *Wheels.* It makes sense eventually to build up a special pair of TT wheels. Here's how. Rims: Mavic gold are the narrowest I've found so far. Hubs: Low flange have less drag than high flange. Campy's are as thin as any and work perfectly, so why switch to those fat sealed-bearing types? Saving weight and maintenance but adding air drag is a step backwards. Spokes: Pino spokes that screw into Pino hubs would save drag at the spoke bends and heads. Failing these, radial spoking on 28-hole low-flange track hubs will turn the most heads and the fewest air molecules. Tires: The skinniest I know of are those Czech Barums.

I suspect that smooth-tread tires catch and fling less air forward as the wheel spins. (Stand in front of someone riding rollers to judge how much air a front tire blows into the slipstream.) If you want to bend the rules, mount a skinny mudguard on your front wheel, back to front so it covers the front of the tire, and claim it's for eye protection against stones, not aerodynamics. You'll win, but they'll never forgive you.

● *Chainwheel.* A great 60-tooth front sprocket, coupled with a 15- to 19-tooth freewheel instead of your 13-17, will give you closer gaps between your gears. But a smaller sprocket saves air drag. The new, undersized Shimano chain/sprocket/cluster rig is a step in the right direction, but at a price. Maybe now other component manufacturers will start wondering why bicycle parts are so bulky.

Those flat-sided Viscount chainwheels *must* be minimum-drag.

● *Cranks.* Like pedals, the crank arms whirl madly around, pushing air forward to frustrate your efforts. Alloy cranks are about ¼-inch wider than steel, so if you stick with steel you save nearly four square inches of surface area.

Don't drill your cranks—or if you insist, drill them from front to back and let a bit of air through. Or, use those cheap steel cranks, round the leading edges, grind the trailing edges to a rounded, aerofoil shape and saw off excess cotterpin length.

Try not to get carried away with a grinder on a pair of brand-new Campy cranks though: there's a lot of stress on a crank when you jump on it at the start of a TT. Maybe you'd better just round the edges and make sure those little crank-bolt covers are screwed in flush.

● *Handlebars.* The lower you mount them, the less stem exposed. The smaller-diameter the tubing, the less drag. (And inexpensive steel bars are thinner than alloy ones.) The narrower, the less drag, but if you're convinced you can't breathe properly unless your bars are 40 centimeters wide, get a pair of narrow, short (low-drop) handlebars and bend them out.

Steel track handlebars make good sense: you're always on the drops in a TT. Why not build up a special TT package of bars, brake and stem, and slip it in before the event?

Note for innovative bike builders: Since the hands in TT are down almost level with the top of the front forks, why should your handlebars have to curve all over the place to reach them? Why not design bars that bolt onto the point where your front brake now bolts? They would stick straight out to the heels of your hands, run forward, curve upwards a bit, and end. You'd be saving the drag from about eight inches of tubing, and trading a whole stem and clamp assembly for just a couple of bolts.

You could remount your front brake either in front, or cobble up a sidepull tucked in behind the front fork stays.

Oh, and oval tubing, please—it has far less drag than round tubing. If some bike manufacturer rises to the challenge, I'll be putting in my order for a TT bike built entirely of oval tubing, with the top tube sloping down to meet the shortest possible head tube. And cables inside the tubing. And . . .

● *Stem.* A recessed Allen bolt on top, of course. That great wedge and bolt hanging down underneath, slap in the slipstream, has got to go. Either grind it all off and braze your steel stem and bars together forever (how often do you want to adjust them anyway?), or find a Cinelli Record road stem, the only streamlined stem made. Otherwise, at least use a stem with the bolt in front of the bars, not underneath.

● *Seat.* A lot of air flows under a seat in 25 miles. Taping in the underside would help but is probably illegal. So let the air flow smoothly in the front and out the back by a little strategic drilling and cutting.

● *Seat post.* If you're choosing a new one, shim the seat tube and fit the skinniest seat post you can buy, preferably grooved. At the upper end, Campy and its copies are more streamlined than the bolt-and-clip type, and the new High-E post looks better still. Use a recessed seat post bolt.

● *Frame.* Dimensions: As a general rule, the more expensive the frame, the worse the air drag. Titanium, aluminum alloy, boron fibers and such exotica usually mean oversize tubing. Some, like the graphite frames, even add extra tubes. For TTs the best possible frame is the narrowest, smallest one. A 21-inch frame pushes a whole inch less of that bulky head tube through the air.

The "steeper" the frame angles (the nearer the head tube is to vertical), the greater the head tube drag will be, and the harder the bike will be to ride in a perfectly straight line when you're exhausted. Any minor differences in frame stiffness only count in a furious stand-up sprint.

Because of the stickiness of air at low speeds, aerodynamic disaster areas such as round objects and bike frame tubing have less drag if they're rough, not smooth. The roughness makes the air slightly turbulent so it doesn't stick so badly. (If you need convincing, shave a tennis ball and then see how far you can hit it compared with a hairy one. Likewise dimpled golf balls: they go five times as far as smooth ones.) So what are all those trackies doing shining up their chromed bikes? Slowing themselves down, that's what.

To dramatically cut the drag on your frameset, spend 90 cents on a roll of 'No-Skid', an adhesive tape impregnated with grit. Stick it along the front half of your forks, head tube, bars, brake levers, seat tube, post, stays, waterbottle, cranks, under the down tube and all over the bottom bracket. The top tube and chain stays, being streamlined, should be kept smooth and polished.

Install an alloy plate behind the head tube, under the top tube. Make it as big as you dare, and paint or tape your racing numbers on each side. The other component whose drag can be somewhat reduced is the rear hub flange, freewheel side. Install the biggest plastic spoke protector you can find.

● *Accessories.* If you use a handlebar-mounted stopwatch, do have the decency to mount it flat, behind the bars. Speedometers, Pacemeters and Digitacs, too, should mount flat behind the bars, clamped along the stem or possibly on the top tube.

Paradoxically, since your speed is 85% a function of air drag, such instruments mainly indicate how the wind is blowing. To hold a given speed reading, you have to keep making wide variations in energy output as the wind shifts.

If instead you decided to hold your energy output at a constant level (on the flat), you would need to keep a constant reading, say 30 m.p.h., on a little air speed indicator. Right? You can get one for $24 from Mehil Enterprises, 5900 Canterbury, Culver City, Calif. It clearly reads 0-38 m.p.h. and weighs two ounces, but has three square inches of frontal area sitting up on your handlebars. Neater is an audio model that complains loudly whenever your relative airspeed drops below

Riding during inclement conditions may necessitate adjustments.

your present speed. It costs $29.95 from Sports Aloft, Box 26, Newcastle, Wyo. 82701. You can mount it straight in front of the head tube.

Ideal would be a crafty electronic minimetronome that you can preset to your chosen cadence and then keep up with. It could buzz when you're below (low tone) or above (high tone) your preset cadence.

Cadence is critical. In your 72-gear, if your average cadence slips down from 110 rpm to 105 (which it easily can without you noticing) your time for the 25 jumps from 1:03:38 to 1:06:40.

● *Fuel.* If you plan to carry food for long events, get Velcro fasteners sewn into your pockets so they don't hang open like drogue chutes. For any event longer than an hour, you'll need to replace fluids and electrolytes as you ride, beginning not when you feel thirsty but within 30 minutes of the start.

Even a 3% drop in body weight cuts your power output by 10%, not to mention your balance and coordination. So carry your bottle of Body Punch either in your middle back pocket or else, for quicker drinks, use an oval-shaped, stream-lined plastic bottle, frame-mounted. You can pick one up at any supermarket, in a choice of white, pink, yellow or blue. When you've used up the dishwashing detergent in it, rinse it out and custom-bend your water-bottle cage to hold it.

Your bike is now set up to give you the full benefit of that surging ¾-horsepower you've trained all these years to produce.

CUTTING BODY AIR DRAG

Three fourths of the air drag problem is that horrible four square-foot area of your body. A reduction of, say, a square foot would rewrite all the record books.

● *Legs.* Don't shave them. Remember the tennis ball. If you fall off your bike, it'll hurt whether your legs are as smooth as a baby's cheek or as hairy as Mario Andretti's. The smoother and better-polished your legs, the slower you'll go. It's that simple.

● *Clothing.* Shirt: Silk is traditionally a low-drag material, but wool is better. Also, tuck in your shirt tail and keep a roll of wide masking tape handy to tape down pockets, number edges and anything else that could flap or ripple.

Shoes: Sandpaper the front of the sole of your TT shoes to a smooth upward curve, and tape down flapping shoelaces.

Head: A cycling cap with the brim turned up must give the most drag, a close crew-cut with a day's chin stubble the least, and a crash helmet probably somewhere in between. The Bell gives excellent protection—but how do you see ahead when you're on the low drops? The Skid-Lid would be fine with an outer skin of thin plastic to smooth its profile. At the Olympics track events a couple of teams had filled in the webs in their leather hairnets with clear plastic. But most of the gold medals went to the gentlemen wearing white, slimline plastic helmets.

The most streamlined helmet of all would be the sharp-tailed Bell Star the downhill skiers use for record attempts. A less extreme version might squeak past the judges . . .

Sunglasses smooth the face a little (thin-rimmed, so you can peer upwards when your head is down). Velcro straps to stop them slipping are worth a few seconds, too. And hand your watch to the timer to hold.

● *Upper body.* A horizontal, flat-backed body profile is so obviously essential in TTs that all training, on road, track or rollers, should be aimed at improving it. There seems little point in getting into shape in the cardiovascular sense, if you get out of shape aerodynamically, developing monstrous thigh muscles and a hump on your back. As the downhill skiers have shown, with their "Egg" and now "Super Egg" positions, suppleness can win races. It takes long flexibility training even to squat in the "Super Egg" position (knees up beside the body, arms out straight in front), let alone ski like that. Addicts of TTS must likewise develop a flexible back, shoulders and neck, to ride stretched-out yet in comfort.

So—lower your stem, then bend your arms until your knees touch your chest on every stroke. You'll need to tilt your saddle downward a shade to avoid the dreaded "numb crotch," and then double-pad your glove palms to avoid numb hands. Your forearms are now horizontal, their drag minimum. (To reduce upper-arm drag you'd have to hold your arms straight ahead like a diver). Keep pedaling in that low-down position and you'll find where the problem lies: your arms collapse. If handlebar drops had a short, fitted extension for you to rest your forearms on, you could to it.

An alternative is straight arms (best for load-bearing) positioned directly in front of your legs, so as to reduce leg drag. This means narrow handlebars set a fork stay level. (Leigh's special Stay Bars are good.)

To get the feel of this revolutionary position, next time you're riding on a smooth road bend down and rest the heel of one hand on the front fork stay, then the other. You'll find you can pedal, and breathe, with an effective handlebar width of two inches. So a foot should be easy. My hunch is that any slight loss in pedaling efficiency would be more than offset by the cut in drag, though only time and time trials will tell. Wind-tunnel testing is useless unless extremely sensitive measurements are made on a standard rider in standard position pedaling at a standard rate, on a dynamometer.

SPECIALIZING IN TIME TRIALS

One-time US Time Trial champion Rick Ball said that anyone so foolish as to give up road racing in favor of time trialing would be specializing in a dead end. He contended that there aren't enough time trials to ride. A strangely defeatist argument.

Organize your own TTs! All you need are two white lines 12½ miles apart and an official with a car or motorbike who can read a split-hand stopwatch. A club TT every Tuesday evening is a superb conditioning workout, and readies the cells for carbo-loading for the following weekend's road race. Or you can use the road race to prep for the TT—it depends on which one you win. Where is the point in specializing in road racing if you're too heavy for climbing, have a dud sprint, or else have strength and endurance but need a while to recover from each break—by which time you've lost your tow?

Alf Engers climbed on his bike one day and, all alone, rode 25 miles in an official world record time of 51 minutes. How does that compare with Merckx winning the Tour de France, towed along by his team, a rotating shift of well-paid assistants who rush ahead up the mountains and are waiting in the next valley to break the breeze for their boss? Is 51 minutes so fast? Well, it puts Engers over two miles ahead of John Howard, and he is strong.

If you decide to specialize in TTs you'll need to build up the best possible TT bike, and as this article shows, that's almost laughably cheap.

The Long Road Against Time
by Martyn Roach

Most cyclists begin their time trialing career with what is considered to be a short-distance effort, such as a 10- or 25-mile event. The "25" is the most popular time trial distance in England, with nearly 4000 competitors in numerous events throughout the country each weekend.

Fewer riders race beyond this distance, which is basically a test of speed. They may compete in the occasional 50-mile time trial, which over the past 10 years has changed from being considered a middle-distance event to being an extension of the 25.

Others like to test themselves further, probing not only their speed but also their stamina and endurance. For these, there are 100-mile, 12-hour and 24-hour races. As distance increases, the emphasis on speed diminishes. I have yet to race in a 24, so I will concentrate on the 100-mile and 12-hour events in this article.

A different type of temperament is required for each of the two time trials. A number of top riders do well at both, but the majority of time trialists only excel at one or the other. I think that this is because the 100 demands an aggressive attitude, while the 12 requires a more patient, self-controlled approach. The fact that in a 12-hour you are riding for a set period of time, which remains the same regardless of how fast you go, ap-

---

Martyn Roach has been a leading British time trialist and road racer for 10 years. In 1968, when he was 21, he broke the British competition records for 100 miles and for 12 hours. He consistently has won British championships ever since, and won both the 100-mile and 12-hour titles in 1976. He works in London for Britain's internal revenue service, and he regularly commutes 15-20 miles each day.

plies mental pressure. Many competitors do not seem able to cope with it.

The severity of the physical effort required to ride a 100 or 12 demands a testy training schedule for several weeks prior to the race. This means that you must decide well in advance when you are going to ride these longer distance events.

Normally, I know in February which races I will be riding in August and September. I usually select the national championship events at both distances, and one other 100. This is usually one of the English classics, such as the Bath Road 100. These would be the only long-distance time trials I would ride in a season, unless my performances in them were particularly disappointing.

The chosen events would be spread over a period of 5-6 weeks, with three weeks separating the first 100 from the 12 and a further 2-3 weeks before the second 100. This spacing is ideal and I would not recommend any smaller gap than two weeks between long-distance time trials.

The first 100 represents an important step in the buildup to the 12. It is not only the biggest effort you are likely to make before it, but also it will serve as an accurate guide for the distance you can hope to cover in the 12-hour.

Training for these events begins from the moment you decide to ride them—if only because you will be thinking about them, thus preparing your mind for the hard work ahead. (Once your mind has accepted what has to be done, in terms of physical effort, then the training will come much easier.)

You will, no doubt, start a general training program prior to the racing season. This program will be supplemented by racing from the start of the season. You should, therefore, be in good shape to start your specific distance training about six weeks prior to the first 100.

During this period you should ride the bike every day. You will be alone in the time trials, so most of your training should be done on your own. It is essential to ride many miles to accustom yourself to being in the saddle for extended periods of time. My recommended weekly schedule follows.

DAY	TIME	SCHEDULE
Mon.	2 hrs.	Steady pace, alone, in low gears (69-72 in.)
Tues.	3 hrs.	In a group of about six. First hour brisk riding, followed by 1½ hours really hard, making as many attacks as you can to push up the pace. Last half hour a steady run-down. Use gears up to about 90 in.
Wed.	3 hrs.	Alone, hard all the way, gears up to 84 in.
Thurs.	3½ hrs.	Alone, hard all the way, gears up to 84 in.
Fri.	2 hrs.	Alone, mainly steady, but with one or two 10-minute bursts in the middle. Restrict gears to mid-70s.
Sat.	2 hrs.	Alone, steady pace in low gears (69-72 in.).
Sun.	Race	Longer road races should be used to build up stamina. They also force you to reach higher speeds than you would reach on your own.

This schedule should be followed until the week before the 100 (or two weeks before the 12). During the week (or fortnight) prior to the event, increase your mileage, especially on the weekend. You should ride about six hours on both Saturday and Sunday, even at the expense of a race. A missed event at this point in your training would not be physically detrimental, and it would probably increase your enthusiasm for the important race ahead. The added confidence provided by longer hours in the saddle will be invaluable.

For the final week, everything you accomplish should be done with the big event in mind. You should go to the start line confident that you are well-prepared and have done everything right. This gives you the best possible chance of success.

The main difference in your final week's preparation is that you should continue to train before a hard 100 (with even an increase in effort if possible) until three days before the race. Before the 12, you should have a relatively easy week. The aim here is to start the event in as fresh of a mental and physical condition as possible.

Your final week's schedules should look like this:

DAY	100-MILE	12-HOUR
Mon.	Two hours in low gears, steady pace, but with a few short bursts.	Two hours, low gears, steady.
Tues.	Three hours in group as before.	Two hours alone at about 20 m.p.h., gears up to 76 in.
Wed.	Four hours alone, very hard, gears up to 84 in.	Two hours, same as above.
Thurs.	Take afternoon off work and do 6-7 hours alone, using gears up to 80 in. Carry food and drink.	Two hours steady, gears 69-72 in.
Fri.	Two hours steady riding, gears to 72; include about six bursts of a mile.	1½ hours gentle riding, gears no higher than 72.

Each evening of this final week, get some extra sleep, particularly on Friday night. Other than your training ride, all you should do on Friday is check over the machine you will be using in the race.

On Saturday, allow yourself to wake up naturally, and spend the whole day at a leisurely pace. After breakfast, make sure you have everything ready for the next day. This includes food, spare wheels and your race clothing.

What food you take will depend on your own preferences. For a 100, you shouldn't need much; certainly no more than you can carry with you. Several glucose tablets, one or two bananas and a drinking bottle (fixed to the frame) should be adequate. Therefore, a helper is not essential in a 100. In England, most riders would not bother with one, although those with a chance of winning would play safe and have spare wheels available in case of flat tires. More importantly, a helper can provide you with regular and accurate time checks on your nearest rivals.

For 12 hours, the amount and varied types of food and drink needed mean that a motorized helper is essential. The basic diet of 12-hour riders in England is rice pudding, usually mixed with canned fruit. You cannot carry this in your jersey pockets, so you must have a helper. He will hand you the food in a suitable container, running alongside while you are on the move. Replenished drinking bottles will be handed up in the same way.

Other favorite foods are fresh peaches, tomatoes, melons, fruit cake and bananas. Chocolate should be avoided and only taken in emergencies because it can cause thirst. Ideally, drinking should be kept to a minimum.

To freshen up (particularly in hot weather) get your helper to hand you plenty of wet sponges. These use up a lot of water, so be sure that you have enough water containers in the car.

Spare wheels are essential, as is a spare bike, if possible. All your hard work could be wasted if you have mechanical failure, but the most important backup of all is your helper.

Usually, you will be riding these long-distance time trials in the summer, so there will be no need to wear anything more than basic racing outfit. If you are really confident, you could wear a silk racing vest in a 100, carrying a small amount of food you require in the pocket of your shorts. But in a 12-hour, always take plenty of food with you in a road jersey, just in case your helper's car has a breakdown.

After a substantial lunch on the day before the race, you

should go out on the bike for an easy hour's ride, using gears of 65-68 inches. You should then relax until supper. This meal should be enormous, as it is the fuel you will be burning in the race next day. Then get to bed early.

If the race is a long way from home, part of Saturday will be spent traveling to the area of the event. Do not travel too late in the day. Plan on reaching your destination with enough time to take a loosening up ride of about 10 miles, in low gears, before the evening meal. And try to arrange accommodations with friends or other cyclists. They will appreciate your feeding requirements (your rather large appetite) and understand why you wish to get to bed early.

On the morning of the race, get up early enough to arrive at the start about 1½ hours before your starting time. You will not need a big breakfast, as you will have stocked up the night before.

Assess the race by determining the wind direction and its strength, and then decide how you will tackle the event. If you can visualize a head wind finish, and you know you are weak in such conditions, save a little strength on the easier stretches. Also, if you have a rival who likes to lead all the way, start fast and try to demoralize him.

I start a 100 at about the same pace I start a 25, but this is after years of experience. A 12-hour requires a more cautious approach because the main target must be to finish. (But do not start too slowly, as time lost early never is completely regained.)

It is best to use 10 gears in long-distance time trials, although many riders in England use only five. It is better to have two chainrings of, say, 50 and 54 teeth with a close-ratio cluster. You are then prepared for any change in the nature of the course or in the weather.

Set out with a definite goal in mind. If you are basically a time trialist who can race 25 miles in the hour, you should be capable of about 4:30 for 100 miles, and around 240 miles in 12 hours. If you are a road man who is accustomed to racing in events from 70-100 miles, you may be capable of about 4:20 for the 100, but you may find it difficult to match the time trialist over 12 hours.

Conversely, the tourist would be slower at 100 miles (4:45:00-5:00:00), but he would be more able to continue at a similar speed for the 12 hours. It is impossible to be too precise, but the beauty of long-distance time trialing is that you can always set new standards for yourself—and beat them.

THE RESULTS

Everybody's
A Winner

In theory, the organization of a time trial is simple. All you need are a course, a timekeeper, a starter and a turn marshall—and the cyclists, of course. But there is a big difference between making the promotion a success and merely doing the least amount of work required.

Organizing a 10-mile time trial may be straightforward. But the longer the event, the more difficult the task becomes. Getting a long-distance trial on the road can be a complex exercise in logistics, coordination and timing.

Sponsorship not only can make an ordinary event special, but also it will make the organization more complicated. So, make sure that your club can do a competent job on a small race before aiming for something bigger.

THE COURSE

The most important factor in a time trial promotion is the selection of a suitable course.

Most riders want a smoothly paved highway that is fairly flat and easy to follow. Race followers and helpers want a safe course with wide roads, good vantage points and good parking facilities. And the police like courses on which other traffic is not inconvenienced by race personnel or competitors.

In addition, your course should be measured accurately.

Because of urban traffic, most courses are in the countryside. Other hazards include traffic signals, railroad crossings, busy intersections and roads that are excessively narrow, hilly or winding.

For a 25-mile course, it is ideal to have a straight, 12½-mile stretch of highway that is divided or wide enough to accommodate traffic overtaking cyclists in each direction. If this is not possible, then a 12½-mile circuit might be the answer, although this limits you to a small number of entrants if you want to avoid overlapping. Another choice is a Y-shaped course on which there are two U-turns.

With the "backbone" of a course established, you must now choose a safe starting point and an equally suitable finish area. It is a good idea to have the start close to a big parking lot: an out-of-town shopping center would suit the purpose if it were closed on Sunday, the traditional day for time trialing. But the competitors must have a quiet road on which to start, with plenty of space for lining up and warming up.

Therefore, do not have the start and finish directly opposite each other on the main strip, but site them both on side roads that will carry the riders off the busier route. Also, a finish line positioned 50-100 yards from parked cars would allow officials to time every finisher without crowd interference, and give riders a clear road on which to slow down.

If you fix the position of the finish in this way, then the course starting point and U-turn would be variable. The critical factor would be the width of the highway and the immediate surroundings at the U-turn. These surroundings would include the distance between the turn and any houses and intersections, and how much visibility is available at the turnaround.

The final choice of the start and turn points should not be made until the actual measurement of the route is accomplished. This should be done by the approved USCF method: ride over the course by bicycle, along a path that will be taken in the race, with a wheel revolution counter fitted on the front forks. The distance in miles is computed by riding the same bike along a measured mile, immediately before and immediately after the course measurement.

For time trials longer than 25 miles, it becomes more difficult to design suitable courses. The best answer is usually a combination of circuits (which should not be covered more than twice at a time) and straight out-and-back legs incorporating U-turns. A distance race, such as a 12-hour or 24-hour, should finish on a circuit that is 10-15 miles long. This will enable an accurate check to be kept on each rider, with the competitor's progress being kept by timekeepers placed every 1-2 miles around the circuit.

No club should take on the promotion of a distance event without first proving it has the capability to successfully run a time trial of less than 50 miles. As the Onondaga Cycling Club in New York has found, the promotion of a 24-hour time trial requires the support of many club members and their friends.

TIMEKEEPING

Accurate timekeeping is a must for a successful time trial. It is simple to time a single rider over a set distance. The difficulties begin when there are dozens of riders in an event, all of whom have to be started on time and checked in accurately at the finish.

For major races, this requires at least two timekeepers—one at the start and one at the end. Each of their clocks must be synchronized and the official at the finish should have two timers in case two riders cross the line within seconds of each other. Also, it is preferable for each timekeeper to have a personal assistant who can act as a second pair of eyes and hands.

Before officiating in an open time trial, a timekeeper should practice by timing small club events. In England, the stringent rules of the Road Time Trials Council (RTTC) require a new timekeeper to act as the assistant to a qualified official for a whole season before the assistant is allowed to take charge of an open event.

But a timekeeper is only as accurate as his timer, which

should be accurately checked and certified before being used for record purposes. And each instrument should be rechecked every year by a qualified watch tester.

The key words for a timekeeper should be punctuality, patience and precision. Without these, he will not be a reliable official.

OTHER RACE OFFICIALS

It is possible for one person to organize a club time trial, but it takes a small army to promote efficiently an important open event. It is still best to have one person coordinating the many different aspects of a promotion, but an organizing committee is desirable also. Each committee member can then be assigned a separate task.

If you are on such a committee, your work will begin in the fall. Decide then what type of time trial your club wishes to promote. Select a course and distance, contact sponsors (if your event is well established) and draw up a rough list of prizes.

Pick a date that does not clash with any area races and fill out an application form to send to the United States Cycling Federation (USCF) for its sanction. Consult your local USCF representative if you have any problems.

One member of the committee should be assigned to producing an entry form which contains all the information about the time trial, including date, time, course, headquarters and prizes. Don't forget the entry fee and the name and address of the official to whom entries should be sent.

Prospective timekeepers should be contacted early, so their valuable services can be booked. Be sure to allow some money in the race budget to pay for the traveling expenses of timekeepers and other key officials.

Another organizing committee member should take care of publicity. His job is to contact local broadcasting stations and newspapers, sending them regular press releases.

If the time trial is sponsored, public relations work is very important. You may want a start and finish area in the center of town, in which case you should seek the cooperation of city officials. Also, you could ask the mayor or a local beauty queen to hand out prizes at the finish.

Reserve the facilities of a center where riders can shower, where snacks can be served and presentations made. Also, use public address equipment to give the event a professional touch.

Another committee member should take care of course details and marshalling. Club members wearing brightly colored vests for safety and recognition can give riders directions. This is better than marking out the course with arrows. So, ensure that enough people are enlisted to accomplish this task.

The start and finish lines should be marked on the road (white tape is very effective) and a black-and-white checkered flag should be fixed at the finish. Assign someone to hold each rider up at the start and have two senior members stationed at the U-turn on the course.

The person who takes charge of the entry forms also should obtain race numbers for the race day and arrange for a well-printed start card. For reasons of efficiency, there should be a two-week cutoff date after which no more applications are accepted. This will guarantee that every rider's name will appear on the official starting list.

The RTTC method for arranging the list of starters is to have the fastest riders on the "10s" (numbers 10, 20, 30, 40, 50 and so on) and the next fastest on the "fives" (5, 15, 25, 35 and so on). The top riders are placed at the back of the field.

Riders should be placed at one-minute starting intervals, preferably with numbers coinciding with the time of day at which they are started. For example, No. 1 would start at 10:01 a.m., No. 2 at 10:02 . . . No. 59 at 10:59, No. 60 at 11:00 a.m., etc.

If the time trial is over a long distance, you will need to appoint checkers to record the numbers of every rider as he passes key points around the course. This information will assist the timekeepers and will ensure that every competitor has covered the full distance.

The chief organizer must check to see every committee member is doing his job correctly, particularly in the weeks and days leading up to the event. The importance of public relations cannot be overestimated. One practice carried out by the Onondaga

CC, for example, is to deliver an explanatory note to every household around the circuit. The residents are informed of race details and times, and are asked to assist by not parking their cars on the highway and by keeping dogs tied up during the race period. To help riders in the dark, they are also asked to turn on any yard lights that will illuminate the roadway.

Once all the entries are in and the list of starters is compiled, it is time to mail start cards and full race details to the riders, race officials, the media and police. This packet, to be mailed at least a week prior to the event, should contain a good map.

Everyone assisting or marshalling should be given specific instructions about his task. During the final days before the race, make sure that everything is double-checked—including the course itself (any road work in progress?), the race headquarters and the associated equipment.

An indispensible aid for spectators and riders is a well-designed, clearly displayed result board. This should be a large, white card listing the starting order (riders and clubs) with spaces for each finishing time. It should be large enough to be read from about 20 feet, and it should be fixed prominently in the finish area—but more than 50 yards away from the actual finish line.

As soon as the last rider has finished, give the timekeepers enough time to check their results and to synchronize timers. Then, announce the results and make the presentations as soon as possible. Later, prepare a comprehensive result list, and have it mailed to every rider and official connected with the event in any way. Needless to say, the media should be kept informed promptly of any developments, with the results phoned in if reporters are not present. It also would be useful to have an official photographer present so that newspapers can be supplied, and so that you have a photographic record of the race.

This could prove extremely useful if you are seeking sponsors for, or official help with, the next year's promotion.

After the race, have a wind-up meeting of the organizing committee and then begin work for the following year. Promoting any event is a case of trial and error, so learn by your mistakes. A high standard of time trial promotion will not only help your own club to obtain greater stature, but also it will contribute to raising the standard of American cycling as well.

STAGE RACES, TEAM TIME TRIALS

The organization of a time trial that forms part of a longer stage race should follow the basic formula outlined above, but it will fall into the general pattern of the overall race promotion. The organization already will exist, so only minor changes will be necessary.

One change is to arrange the starting list (if the time trial is at the end of the race) so that the leading men on the standings are placed at the end of the field. This will give a spectacular climax to the time trial stage.

The distance of the time trial stage should be fairly short, preferably 10 miles or less. This prevents the strong individuals from gaining too great an advantage over the sprinters and climbers.

For a team time trial, starters should be arranged at four-minute intervals (in a four-up trial) or three minutes (for the three). Remember that the time of each team is the time of the third team member to cross the finish line. Also, each team should nominate at least one reserve rider to ensure a full complement at the start.

The advice about wide, traffic-free roads should be followed even more closely in choosing a course for the team time trial.